The Shaping of
Modern French Poetry

The Shaping of
Modern French Poetry

Reflections on unrhymed poetic form
1840 – 1990

ROGER LITTLE

Carcanet Press • Manchester
Alyscamps Press • Paris

First published in Great Britain in 1995 by
Carcanet Press Limited
402-406 Corn Exchange Buildings
Manchester M4 3BY
and in France by Alyscamps Press
35. rue de l'Espérance
75013 Paris

A CIP catalogue record for this book
is available from the British Library.
ISBN 1 85754 189 8 (Carcanet)
ISBN 1 897722 14 1 (Alyscamps)

The publisher acknowledges financial assistance
from the Arts Council of England.

Funded by
THE
ARTS
COUNCIL
OF ENGLAND

Text design by Janet Allan
10 Dale Road. New Mills. Stockport SK12 4NW
Set in 11/13 Bodoni Book by XL Publishing Services. Nairn
Printed and bound in England by SRP Ltd. Exeter

FOR PAT

'thinking, feeling, loving'
(Wordsworth)

Contents

Proem

The immediate stimulus for the present reflections, which I have been mulling over for the last quarter of a century, was a comment made by F.T. Prince in *PN Review* 78 (March/April 1991): 'It seemed to me (and still seems)', he wrote, 'that the Baudelairian tradition of poetry in prose was inextricably bound up with the French language, its inflexions and syntax.' His lack of sympathy with the *Illuminations*, considered by French poets and critics as the high point of Rimbaud's output, seems perverse. His categorisation of them into 'charms or prayers, while others remained baffling or unrewarding', suggests that analysis has failed: magic or dismay are all he is left with, and so he turns to Rimbaud's verse or the hothouse narrative of *Une Saison en enfer* for models and satisfaction. Like so many critics before him, indeed, he spends more time on dating the *Illuminations* than on analysing them. A consideration of whether such escapism is inevitable, particularly for the English-language reader, might lead us towards answers to a number of the difficulties that he or she has coming to terms with the prose poem in particular and modern French poetry in general. The editor of *PN Review*, Michael Schmidt, kindly invited me to share my thoughts with his readers in a series of articles (*PNR* 81, September-October 1991 – *PNR* 92, July-August 1993). Those articles have in turn, with minor modifications, been made into this book, and I have purposely retained an informal approach, wanting to share in a discussion rather than suggest something theoretically definitive but in fact impossible.

The title 'prose poem' suggests a hybrid only if genres are

confused with styles or if, to put it in terms used by George Steiner, the technique of verse is confused with the attribute of poetry. A prose poem should therefore be as susceptible of analysis as a verse poem and leave neither more nor less margin to critics for the unsayable. Certain techniques are knowingly abandoned, the most obvious being rhyme and a certain type of rhythm, while several others dependent on the regularity of line length such as the interplay of line break and syntax (*enjambement, rejet...*) and the consequential rhythmic possibilities are likewise sacrificed. The very constraints of verse as a stimulus to the poet are a form of masochism similarly eschewed by the prose poet. The bulk of the versifier's tools and techniques remain available to him, however, and the choice of prose as a medium allows him to concentrate on such features.

It means that from the outset prose poets, consciously or unconsciously, revelled in metaphor, constructed complex patterns of alliteration and assonance, exploited repetitions and reversals of all kinds, responded to visual stimuli in the very shaping of their texts. So keenly aware were they that the abandonment of traditional verse would be condemned as formlessness that they contrived all possible means of compensation through the techniques available to them. Aloysius Bertrand, in the first volume of prose poems – *Gaspard de la Nuit: fantaisies à la manière de Rembrandt et de Callot*, published posthumously in 1842 – was thoroughly steeped in the Romanticism which insisted on the indissociability of form and content as much as it did on the fascination of the Gothic. It has even been suggested that his fantastic imagery looks forward to surrealism, so extraordinary are some of his juxtapositions. And the relationship between his epigraphs and his texts has been shown to mirror a familiar feature of the seventeenth-century Dutch genre paintings to which he openly alludes: an inscription in stone represented within the painting of a courtyard or a room.

The homage which Baudelaire paid to Bertrand in the prefatory notice to *Le Spleen de Paris* tells of his delight at his discovery

2

in *Gaspard de la Nuit* of the potential of prose as a medium for poetry. If the result is generally less fine and less memorable than his verse poems, the fault should be seen in the practice rather than in the dreamed-of ambition. It might even be that Baudelaire's relative limitations in respect of form – Rimbaud notes that 'la forme si vantée en lui est mesquine' [his much-vaunted form is puny] – made him fail to meet the different but equally stern demands of prose poetry less well than those of verse.

The advent of free verse in the 1870s appears, against this background, as a compromise development, relinquishing fewer of the techniques of traditional verse than prose poetry does and allowing variations of balance between traditional verse and apparent anarchy. Variations of line length and more or less occasional use of end-rhyme are the more obvious features which characterise the work of individual poets... or indeed individual poems, since increasingly the virtues of flexibility in a re-enactment of the subject-matter were recognised and the decorative gave way to the organic.

The road from Paris (I purposely echo the title of Cyrena N. Pondrom's book) was crowded with poets who had heard these new free-verse voices and measured their potential as a resource in English. The same was not true with respect to the far rarer collections of prose poems. Historical chance has therefore played a crucial part in keeping the prose poem as a foreign body, failing to find a champion in the English-speaking world of the calibre of a Pound or an Eliot who so readily espoused the cause of free verse. Eliot's own insistence that free verse should not be confused with bad verse alerts us to the fact that no form can be blamed for a poet's inadequacies. By the same token it is clear that any form properly mastered has the potential for excellence. If someone as alert and sensitive to language as F.T. Prince has missed that potential in the prose poem, it is likely to be true of most readers, and that is indeed my experience. It is not a problem of *which* language is used but a problem of *how* language is used.

The question is, inevitably, complex. Our expectations play an important part, since prose, as M. Jourdain discovered to his surprise, is what we predominantly speak, read and write every day. It has associations of message and report, avoiding ambiguity as much as possible. In the shift from an oral to a literate culture and from a rural to an urban society, it has, through the novel, become the dominant literary form. If poetry were not to become a nostalgic indulgence, it had to *reprendre à la prose son bien.*

I know of no better illustration of that seizure than Rimbaud's *Illuminations.*

Formalism and its offspring structuralism cope well with Mallarmé, whose stock rode high when they were in vogue. The carefully plotted verbal ploys were carefully analysed and the intellectual chemistry split into its component elements for the pure delight of the mind. The high seriousness, even in its finely tuned wit, regaled the scientists at their benches. Rimbaud slipped through their fingers, too elusive, too multiple, too *human.* Too unexpectedly like Mallarmé, also, in his absolute mastery of form.

The magic of *Mystique,* for example, is not beyond analysis, and can serve here to illustrate the degree to which close attention to a prose poem is repaid, a model of rigorous construction to be followed in kind, not in detail, untranslatable but universal.

Sur la pente du talus les anges tournent leurs robes de laine dans les herbages d'acier et d'émeraude.

Des prés de flammes bondissent jusqu'au sommet du mamelon. À gauche le terreau de l'arête est piétiné par tous les homicides et toutes les batailles, et tous les bruits désastreux filent leur courbe. Derrière l'arête de droite la ligne des orients, des progrès.

Et tandis que la bande en haut du tableau est formée de la rumeur tournante et bondissante des conques des mers et des nuits humaines,

PROEM

La douceur fleurie des étoiles et du ciel et du reste descend en face du talus, comme un panier, contre notre face, et fait l'abîme fleurant et bleu là-dessous.

[On the grassy slope the angels turn their woollen robes in the steel and emerald greenery.

Meadows of flame leap up to the crown of the hillock. To the left the ridge is trampled by all murders and battles, and all disastrous noises wend their way. Behind the right-hand ridge, a line of the rising sun's rays, progress.

And while the strip at the top of the picture is formed from the twisting, bounding murmur of sea conches and human nights,

The flowery sweetness of stars and sky and the rest sweeps down opposite the slope, like a basket, against our face, and makes the abyss balmy and blue beneath.]

Were the narrative element (and the cradling curvatures) less present, we would not be lulled into assumptions. The careful balancing of allegorical components defuses our initial surprise at the very ordinariness of the presentation of extraordinary features and events pictured before our eyes. Our eye is guided round the scene, starting at the centre on the slope of the hillock, directed then to left (with its figuration of evil) and right (emblematic of hope) before being shown the scroll at the top of the painting and drawn downwards at the end of the text.

Formally, it has the perfection of a prose sonnet. The voluntary disruptions even seem to underline the fact. The mere fall of a comma proves the 'paragraphs' to be not paragraphs but lines. The first two sentences belong together in their spatial reference and yet straddle a line-break. Prose quatrains and prose tercets emerge clearly, but the technical *tour de force* is the last line. It enacts the curvature of the earlier references (*tournent, mamelon, courbe, tournante, conques*) and of the numerous rounded, often nasalised, vowels. And it does so in the guise of palindromic

5

phonemes around the curved *panier* which lies at its centre: *La douceur – là-dessous; fleurie – fleurant; face – face; comme – contre.* The major words omitted from that list (*des étoiles et du ciel et du reste – l'abîme*) contribute a semantic element to the palindrome and invite us to see a threefold meaning in the word *abîme*: the sea ('the deep') reflecting the stars, a moral abyss in contrast to *ciel* as 'heaven', and the physical gulf which equates below to the immensity of the interstellar cosmos. As to *descend*, it is left to denote the final downward movement of the poet's eye into the infinite depths of a mysterious and perhaps mystical sense of union with the universe in which a medieval painting, it seems, plays the role of catalyst. The repetition of *talus* takes us back to the starting-point of the poem and of the vision to remind us of our bearings and compel us to re-read.

The phonetic texture is so tightly woven that no language other than the original could reproduce it. But can the lessons learnt from analysis not be applied to writing in any language?

Prose throws down the gauntlet to poetry. Even in France, there have been few ready to pick it up, and when they have, the better ones – Reverdy, Breton, Ponge – have had the good sense not to ape Rimbaud but to find their own voice through it. They, like others working through other forms, have not always been successful in dominating the threat of intellectualism, but recent years have seen, alongside the continuing dominance of *vers libres*, the return of rhyme and regular line length and a generally irenic tendency which seems to lead to a sterile angelism and the security of nostalgia. It is as if the very challenge that the prose poem represents has proved too much in its country of origins, so it is scarcely surprising that it should be classified as an alien aberration elsewhere.

The phenomenon of prose poetry helps us to clarify our responses both to the techniques of traditional versification and to the qualities of poetry. It furthermore invites us to reflect on the increased importance of the printed word, visible on the page, in an urban, industrialised society, and a consideration of picture-poems, lettrism, concrete poetry and the like will show that they are the eye-catching manifestations of a profound and important phenomenon in modern French poetry. The undoubted mnemonic attributes of verse seem to relate to a time of orality; the eye has been allowed to redress the balance somewhat for a different age, and developments in the audio-visual media as in modern advertising techniques seem to confirm the trend away from the ear as the sole or principal instrument of verbal memorisation. The very debasement of the techniques of unrhymed poetry in the hoardings and publicity breaks which so offends traditional 'poetic sensibility' is in itself an unwitting homage to its pioneers.

Cratylian Nostalgia

The comments on the prose poem in my introduction require development and further contextualisation, and what follows is an enlargement on propositions made there. Some informality of approach well suits the disentanglement of a complex nexus of interrelated features which to my mind impinge on poetry as it is now conceived and specifically on the shaping of modern French poetry. That the provisional nature of my reflections might give more purchase to constructive criticism is something I welcome. But I should start with an attempt at formulating a principle which guides my reading and then investigate its application to the corpus which particularly interests me.

At the heart of the impulsion towards verbal re-enactment of sense-stimuli which seems to have governed so much of French poetry over the last 150 years lies what I call Cratylian nostalgia. By it I mean the view of language espoused in various founding texts, including the Bible, and discussed in Plato's celebrated Socratic dialogue (known as the *Cratylus* after its much-criticised protagonist), whereby there is a necessary rather than an arbitrary relationship between a word and the object or event it represents. One can readily see the attraction of such a recognisably simplistic view for poets seeking to cope with the breakdown of traditional forms not just of verse but of society itself. It represents a criterion of simultaneous reassurance and adventure in a sea of uncertainty, a veritable *bateau ivre* which generates excitement while guaranteeing a minimum of security. Each poet and ultimately each poem responds to the imperatives of a singular and necessarily complex vision of reality, recreating out of the very arbitrariness of language a necessity, a seeming inevitability, in

8

the relationship between that reality and the words it uses.

In the beginning, the assumption of a necessary link between word and world generated the creation myth, of which footnotes in the New English Bible remind us: 'Then the LORD God formed a man [*Heb.* adam] from the dust of the ground [*Héb.* adamah]' and 'this shall be called woman [*Heb.* ishshah], for from man [*Heb.* ish] was this taken.' The intellectual constructs of millennia are founded on a pun. In the beginning was indeed the word.

Linguists over the centuries have addressed the question with increasing scepticism, culminating in Saussure's assertion of arbitrariness which governs our present linguistic thinking. The last thing the scientists would wish to do is to deny the quite extraordinary disproportion between the collocation of two Hebrew words and their almost universal socio-psychological impact. The linguistician's double-bind is the poet's chance. The coincidental occurrence in two different words of the same phonemes or syllables – *adam* or *ish* in these instances – is made necessary by the simple, even naive, act of creativity, and the reverberations go well beyond the Richter scale, continuing today in feminism's struggle to ensure that women are treated as more than spare ribs.

The poet's task defines itself in this respect as exploring the limits of verbal arbitrariness to seek out and capitalise on chance in his or her affirmation of newly perceived inevitabilities. 'Un coup de dés jamais n'abolira le hasard' [A throw of the dice will never abolish chance] perhaps, but the poet strives towards that paradoxical goal against all the odds. To use another metaphor, suggested by Montherlant in *La Reine morte*, you cannot make a sculpture out of seawater. True as that may be for ordinary purposes, it represents a challenge for the poet: his task encompasses both the impossibility of sculpting water and the unending challenge that notion represents.

In a situation where poets lose sight of poetry's formally exploratory function, a quiet revolution is imperative. Historically, that was

9

the case when, in France, poetry had become indissociably equated with verse during the centuries up to the early nineteenth. And whereas the dynamics of exploration of form and language had sustained it in the early years and brought the notable flowering of the Pléiade in the sixteenth century, the following century saw an increasing tendency to work to formulae. Such exploitation was sometimes brilliantly successful, as in La Fontaine and Racine, but it led to what the French critic Georges Mounin has called the 'Sahara poétique' of the eighteenth century. Only when poetry was dissociated from a particular model of versification, in the 1840s, was it revitalised, both in its rhymed and in its unrhymed forms.

The reasons why it should occur there and then doubtless defy complete enumeration but warrant consideration. For while the predominance of prose might reasonably be construed as a threat and a challenge to poets, there would seem to be other factors, both technological and sociological, to be taken into account. They inevitably overlap, but a cursory glance at the history of printing will lead us into reflections on a shift from orality to literacy, from a rural to an urban society, and on a related change in the nature of the readership which took place around the early nineteenth century.

There are two moments in history when printing took major leaps forward, the first at and after its invention and the second during the industrial revolution. Those were the times of greatest innovation and exploration of the potential of the new technology of the time. Of the latter, which more directly concerns us here, S.H. Steinberg writes in the Penguin *Five Hundred Years of Printing*:

> The turn of the eighteenth to nineteenth centuries marks a decisive stage in the history of printing. It was not a break but rather a sudden leap forward. It affected the technique of printing, the methods of publication and distribution, and the habit of reading. [...] Technical progress, rationalized organization, and compulsory education interacted upon one another. New inven-

10

tions lowered the cost of production; mass literacy created further demands, the national and international organization of the trade widened the channels and eased the flow of books from the publishers' stock departments to the retailers' shelves.

Can it be entirely coincidental that the technical developments of the Renaissance and the industrial revolution should be followed immediately in France by the greatest periods of poetry? That the excitement generated by new printing techniques and the prospect of enlarged audiences should stimulate an urgency, a vibrancy, which we still feel? Or that rotary presses should represent progress in literacy and information for the masses and the triumph of prose, which poets would adopt so as to exploit its oblique, hitherto untapped potential and subvert its communicative assumptions?

Increasing literacy and urbanisation brought fundamental changes to an oral and rural society. The number of those able to read increased greatly, the major moments in this development being marked by the shifts from the production of manuscripts to that of printed material, from wood to metal type, and then, massively, in the eighteenth century, with the introduction of stream-driven presses. Symbiotically, printing both fostered and benefited from the spread of education.

The particular habit of reading inculcated by the late eighteenth-century innovations seems to have favoured prose: the relative cheapness of new methods encouraged quantity and ephemerality. The spread of newspapers, the ascendancy of the novel, the huge increase in the literature of information, delivered more and more regularly in weekly or monthly instalments, these have a family likeness and suggest the appealing but ultimately misleading paradox that more generalised literacy involved a devaluation of words. In the realm of education, the reactionary argument that more means worse signally fails to take account of massive benefits: where would so many of us be now without the 1944 Education Act? The extension of literacy among the developing middle classes of the 1800s can scarcely be considered a devaluation, even if losses were involved. What is important for my present argument is the change it brought about in the approach to words. Performance gave way to perusal.

By definition, more eyes were trained on the page. The private scanning of words on the increasingly familiar printed page gained ground over the shared community of heard recital or narrative. One reads a novel alone in silence. However much a novel may be the evocation of a society, dependent for its verisimilitude on a fictional representation of a credible world of its own, it is in practice focused on and intended for the individual. Similarly, a newspaper is as much a screen from others in a literal sense as one on which those others are metaphorically projected. Literacy gained at the expense of orality, just as the town extended its tentacles to the detriment of the countryside, and solitude tended to give way to isolation. Rousseau's distinction, in his *Essai sur l'origine des langues*, between sight, space, gesture and concrete object on the one hand, and sound, time, words and abstract notion on the other, broke down when the printed word, a spatially visible representation of sound, became the prime vehicle for exchange. Only the active poet, Baudelaire suggests in 'Les Foules' (first published in 1862), can be – to revivify the phrase – *by* himself, alone and yet multiple, in a crowd, converting isolation back into solitude: 'Qui ne sait pas peupler sa solitude, ne sait pas non plus être seul dans une foule affairée. Le poète jouit de cet incomparable privilège, qu'il peut à sa guise être lui-même et autrui.' [Anyone who cannot people his solitude cannot be alone in a bustling crowd either. The poet enjoys the incomparable privilege of being able to be himself and someone else at the same time.] The active poet was also armed to capitalise on and break free from the banalisation of the printed alphabet.

Artists responded in different ways to the challenge represented by the industrial and commercial centres which are our modern cities. On the whole, English-language poets needed prompting by their French counterparts, and Baudelaire's role was crucial in this

12

respect. But even Bertrand's espousal of prose in *Gaspard de la Nuit* (1842) coincides with his choice of Dijon as a setting. Historians of the *poème en prose* have often pointed to Rousseau and Chateaubriand as influential stylists, yet a distinction must be made between their poetic prose and the prose poem as such, for however difficult it may be to define the latter, it is clearly distinct from the former. It is notably a synchronic entity (as is a painting, something we shall explore further), not a purple patch in a less highly coloured context. Their subject matter too was different from what became dominant in the *poème en prose* : the focus through which they fostered a new sensibility was nature. Only grudgingly and occasionally did they acknowledge any virtue in metropolitan or industrial society, as when, in the seventh *Rêverie*, Rousseau stumbles across a stocking factory during a solitary walk through wooded hills. Baudelaire pointedly selects an urban setting for the 'description de la vie moderne' of his prose poems collected as *Le Spleen de Paris* (even if some are situated elsewhere), whereas only some of *Les Fleurs du Mal* are set in the city. Yet it should be remembered that Bertrand's Dijon was the ancient city, distanced in time, and that Maurice de Guérin's *Le Centaure*, published in 1840, is set in a mythological countryside as fanciful as any one might imagine.

The emergence of the prose poem suggests an awareness, though never formulated as such, of the inappropriateness of rhyme, that key factor in the *hearing* of a poem, to conditions in which the text was primarily to be *seen* on the page. Rhyme becomes more and more redundant the further poetry is removed from oral/aural transmission. The use of prose for poetry derives in some measure from an implicit recognition that verse no longer corresponded to the circumstances of a changed readership, and represents a radical departure, in contradistinction to traditional verse forms. (Rhythm is a far less central factor in French, which carries no tonic accent, than in English, where the development of blank verse and eye-rhymes, virtually unknown in French, betokens a shift of interest away from rhyme as such.)

13

The consequent importance of the physical disposition of a text on the page is evident. The unique objects of beauty painstakingly penned by myopic scribes had given way to wood-block printing which could accommodate pictures as well as words. Aesthetic satisfaction was in time transferred to the type-face itself, so going hand in hand with technological progress, and to its presentation on the page. In more expensive and specialised books fine printing was accompanied by woodcuts or engravings. Of course, the potential of the hand-printed page has fascinated the artisan printer-poet, from Geoffroy Tory to William Blake and beyond, but whereas the former was exploiting the latest technology, the latter was consciously turning his back on it. Only with the introduction of steel engraving in the nineteenth century did illustration become sufficiently banal to warrant reflection as to how to revitalise a jaded aesthetic sense.

The very variety of forms in modern French poetry both resulted from the new awareness and practice of flexibility and sensitised verse-poets to the spatial virtues of their own products. It is not only bibliophiles who are alert to the differences of effect between a sequence of lyric poems given a page each with generous margins and the same sequence cramped nose to tail with no space for the resonances to develop in the reader's imagination.

With the radical innovation of the *poème en prose*, verse had to look to its laurels. The playful acrostic technicalities of the fifteenth-century *Rhétoriqueurs* were remembered by the poets who were writing under the impact of the second great wave of development in printing. In the 1840s, art for art's sake primarily meant craft for craft's sake, the more social forms of aestheticism coming only towards the end of the century. Gautier chiselled away at his verse, relishing diffficulty and producing triumphs of form: 'Oui, l'œuvre sort plus belle / D'une forme au travail / Rebelle.' [Yes, art benefits / From a form that's / Hard to work.] Parnasse followed with a similar emphasis, and typically Mallarmé's verse, in a shipwreck of syntax, has the formal complexity of a Fair Isle knitting pattern.

14

Such a development runs parallel to the explorations of unrhymed poetry in French nineteenth-century poetry and seems to me to represent a different and equally valid reaction to essentially similar data: the hegemony of prose and the challenge of increased literacy. Each development in its own way called into question existing assumptions about the nature of poetic form. In the process, each stretched the limits of poetry, but the prose poem represented the more radical investigation of form, concentrating on the organic rather than on the decorative.

One hundred and fifty years later, this key issue prompts the present musings on its status and importance. I am persuaded that its flexible embodiment of the principle of Cratylian nostalgia revitalised French poetry in a crucial way, the repercussions of which are still being felt in the sense of appropriateness as an essential criterion for poetry. This involves techniques of appropriation and re-enactment which seem, on the basis of factors I have intimated, to be particularly governed by visual features, and I shall tease these questions out on the basis of significant examples in the course of this study. The central view of each work as a new beginning, felt so keenly by the writer, pen poised over blank paper, justifies investigation and an attempt at explanation by the critic. Julian Barnes made the comment in a 1991 *Observer* interview that 'in order to write, you have to convince yourself that it's a new departure for you and not only a new departure for you but for the entire history of the novel.' It may be daunting to have to consider each text as a new departure, but we are specifically invited to do so by Francis Ponge who, more clearly than anyone, enunciates and applies the principle of *adéquation* and insists on the existence of 'une rhétorique par poème' [one rhetoric per poem].

Before looking more closely at his contribution and that of some of his predecessors, however, there is more to be said about the evolution of unrhymed poetry and about the relationship between the visual and the verbal in modern French poetry in general.

Rhythms of Re-enactment

Any idea which runs counter to current thinking is bound to prompt enthusiasm from radicals and dismissal from reactionaries. Equally, however, it should not be imagined that Cratylian nostalgia sprang up, as it were, fully clad, after lying dormant for centuries, when the first prose poem was published. The principle of a shaping force for poetry other than the conventions of versification had disappeared underground for so many generations that when it re-emerged after ages of neglect it did so very tentatively. Poets showed their awareness of the principle long before the critics, but at first the point was made within the forms of traditional verse. So André Chénier, who was to die on the scaffold in the Revolution, could write both that 'Chaque chanson nouvelle a son nouveau langage' (which is absolutely central to the principle of re-enactment) and that 'L'art ne fait que des vers; le cœur seul est poète' [Verses may be made by art; poetry requires a heart] (which unhappily steers the concept towards Romantic self-indulgence). In *De l'Allemagne* (1810), Mme de Staël records the sense of unease brought about by the new awareness: 'Le despotisme des alexandrins force souvent à ne point mettre en vers ce qui serait pourtant de la véritable poésie.' [Alexandrines are so despotic that one is often inclined not to put true poetry into verse.] With *Les Orientales* (1829), Hugo flexed his versifying muscles to show an important lead in the practice of verse adapting to its subject-matter so as to produce a total effect with a sense of absolute *rightness* which went beyond the crude critical division of form and content. His choice of exotic material went some way towards 'legitimising' the striking elasticity of his verse forms and making them more acceptable to a public still mesmerised by generic conventions. And the shorter the line, the more a sense of the poem's verticality impinged, stressing a spatial dimension which had been largely lost from view during two centuries of domination by the alexandrine. Hugo would go on, in his *Journal de 1839*, to suggest symbolic or pictorial values for all the letters of the alphabet and, in his essay on translators, to stress that 'forme et fond adhèrent au point que dans beaucoup de cas, le fond se dissout si la forme change.' [Form and content are so indissociable that in many cases the content dissolves if the form changes.] As so often in other respects with Hugo, however, he proves a dubious ally of the organic principle in poetry since, paradoxically, his talent in verse drew him towards traditional forms and the merely decorative.

The choice of rhyming verse by subsequent poets should not be seen as unthinking conservatism, even though in mere versifiers it may well have been that. The new awareness of a need for 'une rhétorique par poème' led to particular attention being given to phonetic texture. In late 1835, Vigny voiced appropriate disdain for 'la faculté mécanique de la poésie, celle qui fait le rimeur mais non le poète' [the mechanical faculty of poetry, that which makes the rhymester rather than the poet], but had none the less already affirmed that 'il n'y a point de Poète en prose' [there is no such thing as a Poet in prose] and held firmly to the traditional view when he later wrote: 'La poésie n'est que dans les vers et non ailleurs' [Poetry resides in verse and not elsewhere]. The more progressive attitude was becoming established, however, expressed in formally alert poems both in verse and prose. An interesting echo may be found in Mérimée's well-known tale *Colomba* of 1841, in which a sympathetic comment on the new poetry is found: 'Au lieu d'être en vedette, les vers se suivaient sur la même ligne, tant que la largeur de la feuille le permettait, en sorte qu'ils ne convenaient plus à la définition connue des compositions poétiques: "De petites lignes, d'inégale longueur, avec une marge de chaque côté."' [Instead of standing out, the lines ran on as far as the width of the paper would allow, so that they didn't correspond any longer to what one thinks of as poetic compositions, 'short lines, unequal in length, with a margin on either side'.] It is just that laundry-list view of verse which was happily becoming increasingly unacceptable as the new (but of course very old) principle of appropriateness gained ground, allowing Nerval in his turn to acknowledge that 'il est possible de ne pas rimer en poésie.'

Michel Foucault saw the threshold between classicism and modernity in literature as being 'un acte d'écrire qui ne désigne plus rien que soi' [an act of writing which designates nothing else but itself]. I believe this to be another way of expressing the re-enactment which concerns us here. When language draws attention to itself, there is inevitably the authorial self-consciousness which we associate with modernity (as in Diderot or Sterne) and indeed with modernism. When language becomes its own finality and is recognised as having an existence independent of, although necessarily nourished by its conventions of meaning, its social performance and its designation of reality, it allows all its components to function interactively beyond both genre and dictionary.

The way in which this recognition is reached in different languages is quite properly and understandably different. If one considers English and French, it is clear that the nature of rhythm in the two languages goes a long way to explaining the separate developments in poetry since the Romantics and to consequent critical responses. On the one hand, tonic stress fixed immutably for each word; on the other, weaker tonal stress governed by syntactical sub-units. In English, so many feet per line, designated by Greek terms – iamb, dactyl and so forth – which specify the relationship between stressed and unstressed syllables; in French, an arithmetic of syllables, the twelve of the alexandrine being the most familiar, but no predetermined regularity (or irregularity) of rhythm within the line. Such, at least, and very briefly, is the accepted wisdom.

It is clear, however, that during the Renaissance classical models were much in the minds of the poets and that the very challenge of excellence represented by the ancient masters

18

continued to haunt poets for centuries to come. The homage is
overt in the choice of Greek and Roman mythological subjects; it
is hidden in the matter of French versification, and the manuals
on the subject tend inevitably to over-simplify. In endeavouring to
explain to generations of students how reams of alexandrines are
not rhythmically boring, it seems essential, if obvious, to observe
that simple arithmetic is not enough. The grammatical sub-units
of French create the equivalent of iambs, anapests and paeons, so
weaving a complex tissue of cross-rhythms which, in the case of
dramatic verse, an actor will recognise and exploit. In short, just
as happens in English, the principle of a basic regularity of beat,
with modulations for appropriate effect, and with the consequent
de-emphasising of unstressed syllables, comes into play. At its
crudest, one can say that the importance to be attached to a word
in French verse is in inverse proportion to the number of syllables
in the sub-unit in which it figures. And always, unless there is a
reversal of stress for special emphasis, the final syllable of such a
group carries the tonal stress (rising except at the close of a state-
ment, when it falls).

Such rhythm, even if less strongly marked than in English, is
the clearest guide to the relative importance given by the writer to
the various components of the line, and the following couplet
from Racine's *Phèdre* offers a clear example:

> Le voici. Vers mon cœur tout mon sang se retire.
> J'oublie, en le voyant, ce que je viens lui dire.

> [He's here. All my blood flows back to my heart.
> I forget, seeing him, what I have to impart.]

Phèdre catches her breath as she sees Hippolyte on stage for the
first time. Her attempts at self-control show in the 3 / 3 / 3 / 3
division of the first of these lines and start breaking down in the
second, with its exponential 2 / 4 / 6 expansion of the number of
syllables and consequent reduction of importance from the

19

crucial 'J'oublie' which, in theory at least, would occupy the same amount of time as the whole of the second hemistich, 'ce que je viens lui dire'.

An extreme if rare case, arguably going so far as to let a monosyllable fill the time of the other eleven syllables in the line, matches the intensity of emotion felt in Corneille's *Horace* when Camille curses her brother's killing of her foreign fiancé in the name of Rome:

> Rome, l'unique objet de mon ressentiment!
> Rome, à qui vient ton bras d'immoler mon amant!
> Rome qui t'a vu naître, et que ton cœur adore!
> Rome enfin que je hais parce qu'elle t'honore
>
> [Rome, the only thing that I resent!
> Rome, from whom your arm my love has rent!
> Rome who bore you and whom you adore!
> Rome whose honour to you I deplore!]

At the beginning of that same scene, Horace had proudly announced his triumph in lines where the key word 'bras', the very instrument of that triumph, weaves in and out:

> Ma sœur, voici le bras qui venge nos deux frères,
> Le bras qui rompt le cours de nos destins contraires,
> Qui nous rend maîtres d'Albe; enfin voici le bras
> Qui seul fait aujourd'hui le sort de deux États; ...
>
> [Camille, this arm has our brothers' vengeance wrought,
> This arm divergent destinies has fought,
> And Alba now is ours; this arm the fates
> Has sealed, in single combat, of two States.]

The predictability of line-length, underpinned by the coupling of rhyme, allows the actor to convey the counterpoint of line and grammar. Even so, one *sees* in print the displacement of 'le bras' relative to the alexandrine. Where line-length is unpredictable, the impact of the visual is intensified relative to the acoustic, as William Carlos Williams displays in a verse from 'To a Poor Old Woman' who is savouring fruit, enacted as the poet savouring words:

> They taste good to her
> They taste good
> to her. They taste
> good to her.

Or again, even more insistently and wittily, as if a ripple of murmured repetitions of the gentleman being announced were going round the assembled company, e. e. cummings in poem 9 from *No Thanks*:

> The (The president The
> president of The president
> of the The) president of
> the (united The president of the
> united states The president of the united
> states of The President Of The) United States

> Of America...

What is clear at least in French is that the arithmetical principle is in practice merely a frame against which the counter-principle of prosody can ebb and flow. I see nothing to suggest that French poets in verse worth their salt ever lost this sense of a double tradition, one syllabic and the other metrical. The awareness of it disappeared, however, when poetry disappeared, in the eighteenth century, and does not seem to have resurfaced until Claudel championed 'l'iambe fondamental' [the basic iamb] at the beginning of this century. Even so, because of the nature of the French

21

language, an effect like that of a stress falling on silence, such as Milton achieves in the opening line of *Paradise Lost*, is simply not available to the French poet. Yet that very line shows how similar in the two languages is the relationship between the number of syllables in a word-group or foot and the importance attached to the unit with the fewest words:

> Of man's first disobedience, and the fruit
> Of that forbidden tree...

The whole epic poem is there in embryo, but the quintessential word is 'first', with its neighbouring words set apart by the stressed pause on the comma. Next in importance is the foot 'Of man's', again for reasons entirely justified by the theme of the poem. A hierarchy of importance is thus established prosodically, whether in English or in French, to enhance or nuance our understanding of the lines.

Such a brief excursion into the traditional nature of French verse from a slightly unusual angle is intended above all to suggest both the differences from English, which tend to be well known to the point of overstatement, and certain underlying similarities between the two prosodies. It seems to be the nature of rhythmic stress in English which contributed to the eschewing of prose-poetry in the nineteenth century, the more conservative attitude to form, as evinced by Coleridge, maintaining the upper hand partly through the entirely legitimate argument that constraints can be a stimulus to invention. Baudelaire was fully aware of this, observing in his *Salon de 1859*: 'jamais les prosodies et les rhétoriques n'ont empêché l'originalité de se produire distinctement. Le contraire, à savoir qu'elles ont aidé l'éclosion de l'originalité, serait infiniment plus vrai.' [Prosody and rhetoric have never prevented anyone producing something distinctly original. The opposite, namely that they have encouraged the flowering of originality, would be infinitely more true.] Yet he was prompted to compose *Le Spleen de Paris* where his English-language counterparts felt no such urge. George Moore could still write, in his *Confessions of a Young Man*, in a parallel and no less valid argument whereby freedom requires a yardstick by which it can be measured, that 'you must have rules in poetry, if it is only for the pleasure of breaking them,' adding with dubious taste and accuracy: ' just as you must have women dressed, if it is only for the pleasure of undressing them.'

The question of rhythm clearly impinges on the development of free verse and became a matter of particular concern towards the end of the nineteenth century, when Pater's notion that poetry aspires to the condition of music held particular sway. Mallarmé is quoted by Mondor, his biographer, as remarking that 'toute phrase ou pensée, si elle a un rythme, doit le modeler sur l'objet qu'elle vise à reproduire' [every sentence or thought, if it has a rhythm, should model itself on the object it seeks to reproduce]. Rhythm is understood here not simply as relating to a pattern of words but also, by extension, to other phenomena, something which Henri Meschonnic has developed in recent years into a theory of bewildering idiosyncrasy. Commenting on *Un coup de dés*, Mallarmé acknowledged the danger of losing rhythm more strictly related to poetry for the sake of creating particular visual effects, and Pound (who has been so acutely observed as a 'sculptor' of poetry by Donald Davie) was to echo this doubt when he suggested that 'poetry atrophies when it gets too far from music.' Neither statement, however, nor the familiar primacy of music in Symbolist poetry, should blind us to the interest shown in visual or sculptural form revealed in so many ways among nineteenth-century French poets. Indeed, Laforgue once wrote in a letter to a friend that 'c'est par l'œil qu'arrive bien un peu le rythme d'abord' [it is through the eye that, to some extent, rhythm first comes], showing once again the importance of the shift from an oral tradition to the printed page.

Although there is no neat pattern of chronological development from the extrinsic to the intrinsic in respect of an interest in matters visual, that tendency might be seen as a general shift of

23

balance in parallel to the shift from the decorative to the organic. Aloysius Bertrand's overt fondness for Dutch painting and Callot's etchings as evidenced in *Gaspard de la Nuit* finds echoes in Baudelaire, for example, in a variety of forms of expression. Able to satisfy his interest in painting openly in his *Salons*, he could tease out some of the psychological implications of his visual sense in his poetry (and especially in his prose poems) and reserve a more integrated mode for his *transpositions d'art*. Gautier's training as an art historian refined his sensibility to the visual arts and again allowed him both to make analytical observations and to allow some of his highly-wrought poems to reflect their source in a particular work of art. The excellent study of *Pictorialist Poetics* by David Scott gives all the detail one could wish in these matters. One notes in addition, however, the plethora of volumes of poetry in the mid-nineteenth century which refer more or less directly to the visual arts: *Fresques et bas-reliefs, Tableaux et pastels, Mosaïques, Eaux-fortes, Aquarelles, Dessins à la plume, Fusains, Sanguines* and so forth. The fashion, even when somewhat mindlessly followed as is so often the case with fashions, suggests a preoccupation with the visual which was to bear such spectacular fruit at the end of the century and beyond. For by then the flood of free verse, heralded by Rimbaud's 'Marine' and 'Mouvement' in the early 1870s and ushered in by Marie Krysinska, Gustave Kahn and Jules Laforgue in the 1880s, had added an important new set of possibilities to the shaping of poetry.

The fact that the advent of *vers libres* followed that of the prose poem by some thirty or forty years (depending on whether one considers the then unknown 'Marine' and 'Mouvement' to count as the beginning of *vers libres*, or whether instead to consider the 1880s as the effective starting-point) suggests that some causal relationship might be sought. If it is to be found, I believe it to lie in the sense of appropriate re-enactment on the one hand and in a spirit of compromise on the other. *Vers libres* are, after all, a kind of half-way house between traditional verse and the prose poem, and other compromise forms would follow. Not long afterwards, for example, Claudel would reintroduce the *verset* and the *laisse*, though in each case with new meanings ascribed to old phenomena, just as *vers libres* had formerly described the form of La Fontaine's *Fables*. The biblical *verset* was, in Claudel, governed by other forces, which we can investigate later; the medieval *laisse*, grouping lines ending with the same assonance, was now applied to the groupings of such series of *versets* between, so to speak, stanza or paragraph breaks. But the prose poem too had found its most brilliant exponent in Rimbaud, whose *Illuminations* were written in the early 1870s but not published until 1886, and Mallarmé's *Un coup de dés jamais n'abolira le hasard* exploded on to the pages of a magazine in 1897, a year before his death. These texts (and particularly the former because of the far less obvious nature of their formal concerns) must be given particular attention, for their influence has been immense. Despite all the manifest differences between them, *Un coup de dés* and *Illuminations* join forces in representing high points in the shaping of modern French poetry precisely because they utilise form in extreme as well as exciting ways which, for all their apparent novelty, tap ancient traditions in exploiting the principle of organic appropriateness.

25

Rainbow Rimbaud

The supreme examples in French poetry of the totally mastered self-designating act of writing are Mallarmé's verse and Rimbaud's prose poems. So long considered at opposite poles, partly no doubt because of the very obvious differences of presentation, but partly too, I suspect, because literary biography is an appealing substitute for literary analysis, both take to an extreme the desire to create complex artefacts which, in text and texture, re-enact the totality of a mood-event (the two being inseparable) while contributing to the further dynamic re-enactment of that mood-event in the reader's mind.

It is understandably easier to recognise Mallarmé's mastery than Rimbaud's because he generally works within a familiar formal tradition. Like Valéry after him, however, he did make occasional excursions into prose poetry. The example of Baudelaire, with a major collection in both verse and prose, was that of a colossus straddling the apparent abyss. But it is clear that Mallarmé's inquiring mind led him to range widely over the potential field and benefit from his reflections to the point where, near the end of his life and the century, he produced the epoch-making *Un coup de dés jamais n'abolira le hasard*. I shall return to this extraordinary spatial poem to consider its antecedents and impact in the next chapter: suffice it to say for the moment that it takes a place of honour in the development of awareness of organic *adéquation* as a principle for poetry.

In his parallel exploratory adventure, Rimbaud produced the first *vers libres*, as we have seen, at a date which cannot be determined precisely but which is likely to be 1872. They seem to me to be an integral part of that impulse towards Cratylian nostalgia which I have already evoked: an impulse among modern poets to prefer not to acknowledge the division between words and things which modern linguisticians, agreeing with Hermogenes, insist is there. 'Marine' and 'Mouvement', somewhat arbitrarily gathered in *Illuminations*, preceded by a decade the great flowering of that form which has so dominated European poetry in the twentieth century.

Rimbaud's contribution to that development is, as I have already suggested, remarkable but far less obvious. The example given in my proem, that of 'Mystique', shows in a nutshell the capacity of prose both to exploit the techniques familiar in verse, with the major exception of regular rhyme, and to cover its tracks so that our daily habit of reading prose blinds us to its capacities for becoming poetry. A century passed during which nobody, it seems, noticed the palindromic ploy of the closing line or was therefore in a position to tease out the consequences for the text as a whole or indeed for our view of Rimbaud. The problem for the critic is that when each new poem represents a new beginning, he too has to start again to discover the features and forces which govern the writing of that particular poem. It is not a question of replacing the mould of verse by some other mould, even if there are recurrent patterns which contribute on different occasions to different effects.

Once one perceives the balanced finesse of 'Mystique' depending not just on semantic elements but on stylistic features too, the turn of the prose sonnet ('Et tandis que...') being placed as tradition would have it at the opening of the sestet, one cannot help noticing that while not a single one of the many sonnets Rimbaud wrote bears the title 'Sonnet', this is precisely the title of one of the prose texts collected under the general heading 'Jeunesse'. Is it mere chance that the manuscript sets the text out in fourteen lines, the first four of which rhyme (albeit in a quite unclassical way: 'chair', 'verger; – o', 'prodiguer; – o', 'terre')? Mere chance that a series of internal rhymes seems to bind the text together and even to suggest alternative line-breaks which would place the turn ('Mais à présent...') after a hypothetical octave of lines which

toy with the traditional alexandrine? Mere chance that the phonet-
ic focus shifts from [eR] and [oR] in the 'octave' to [ãʃ] and [wa] in
the 'sestet', with 'descendance' standing in anticipation of the
latter and 'force' near the end urging us back to the beginning, a
yin-yang totality with dots in the opposite colour?

Closures that are at the same time openings are a familiar
enough feature of poetry, but they assume particular importance
when a prose poem seeks to stand outside the temporal, sequen-
tial assumptions of narrative. Rimbaud is adept at producing
endings which not merely fail to conclude but positively thrust us
back into the text for a further exploration of its resonances. A
locus classicus occurs at the end of 'Les Ponts', where 'Un rayon
blanc, tombant du haut du ciel, anéantit cette comédie' [A shaft of
white light, falling from the highest point in the sky, abolishes this
comedy]. Coming after a text which presents 'un bizarre dessin de
ponts' [a bizarre drawing of bridges] and which remains for sever-
al sentences within the assumed confines of a black and white
drawing, the bright shaft of white light shines down in a way
which can well be interpreted within a known graphic tradition.
That its brilliance should somehow abolish the scene by blinding
us is again within the bounds of familiar logic. What disrupts
these assumptions is the final word: 'comédie'. Unprepared for its
abrupt dismissiveness, we have to reinvestigate the text to pene-
trate its meaning. The importance of elements in it which make it
impossible to see it as mere description of what might be a
Piranesi etching (I think, for example, of plate VII of his *Carceri*)
then impinges with greater force. To the black and white visual
shots, music of a strangely kinetic kind is added. Then a red jack-
et stands out against the grey; water is tinged with blue; and the
three estates in turn – people, aristocrats and church – are given a
brand of music each in rapid, interrogative succession: 'Sont-ce
des airs populaires, des bouts de concerts seigneuriaux, des
restants d'hymnes publics?' [Are they popular tunes, snatches of
lordly concerts, the remains of public anthems?] The drawing has
come to life, and with representative society jostling around the

band comes the symbolism of the Revolutionary flag: blue, white and red. Description becomes 'comédie humaine' in a manner both oblique, rapid, dense and disarticulated which runs counter to our assumptions about communicative prose.

Time and again we are thrown back provocatively on our ignorance. Negatives abound as the blank page reasserts its right not to explain. Some examples: 'la Reine, la Sorcière qui allume sa braise dans le pot de terre, ne voudra jamais nous raconter ce qu'elle sait, et que nous ignorons' [the Queen, the Sorceress who brings her embers to life in an earthenware pot, will never tell us what she knows, and what we are ignorant of] ('Après le déluge'); 'La musique savante manque à notre désir' [Our desires lack skilful music] ('Conte'); 'Je suis réellement d'outre-tombe, et pas de commissions' [I am genuinely from beyond the tomb; no commissions] ('Vies'); 'Non! nous ne passerons pas l'été dans cet avare pays où nous ne serons jamais que des orphelins fiancés. Je veux que ce bras durci ne traîne plus *une chère image*' [No! we shall not spend the summer in this miserly country where we are doomed to be nothing but orphans affianced. I don't want this sturdy arm to drag *a beloved image* along any more] ('Ouvriers'); 'En tout cas, rien des apparences actuelles' [In any case, nothing of present appearances] ('Jeunesse'); 'Mais plus *alors*' [But no more *then*] ('Dévotion'). Even where the syntax is not negative, the sense may well be, though it can equally well, in many cases, support both a negative and an affirmative reading simultaneously: 'J'ai seul la clef de cette parade sauvage' [I alone hold the key to this wild parade] ('Parade'); 'Arrivée de toujours, qui t'en iras partout' [Come from always, you will go everywhere] ('À une raison'); 'Voici le temps des *Assassins* ' [Now is the time of the *Assassins*] ('Matinée d'ivresse'); 'Au réveil il était midi' [When he woke it was midday] ('Aube'); 'Un souffle disperse les limites du foyer' [A breath dispels the limits of the hearth] ('Nocturne vulgaire'); 'Rouler [...] aux tortures qui rient, dans leur silence atrocement houleux' [Roll on [...] to laughing tortures, in their atrociously heaving silence] ('Angoisse'). Elsewhere, open questions hold us

29

in suspense or defiant claims make us bridle and search for a justification. In short, Rimbaud is purposely playing with our expectations and deploying the panoply of ambiguity and ambivalence not merely in individual words, but also in phrases, sentences and poems. The shimmering surface texture is at one with the complex tangle of meaning and counter-meaning which critics are at pains to unravel.

As Mary Douglas observed in *Purity and Danger*, 'it is not always an unpleasant experience to confront ambiguity', making the obligatory glance of homage towards Empson, to conclude: 'we enjoy works of art because they enable us to go behind the explicit structures of our normal experience. Aesthetic pleasure arises from the perceiving of inarticulate forms.' To the last two words should be added, I believe, the adverb 'apparently', having no quarrel with the concept of articulate form but much more with the habits of conservatism and sheer laziness which are the majority response in any age to contemporary art. In fairness, however, it must be acknowledged that freedom of any kind is one of the most difficult things to analyse as well as to control. The criteria for judging free verse (and here I include all forms of unrhymed verse) have each time to be established afresh before the evidence of the individual case. The importance of the principle of organic re-enactment is that it provides a possible critical framework within which our poetic sensitivities can apply themselves to the particular features of a given poem.

Given the spatial and visual dimension which I see as being of special importance in the development of unrhymed poetry, it is worth reflecting that certain types of 'peintures idiotes' and 'enluminures populaires' which Rimbaud declares himself to be fond of in the 'Alchimie du verbe' section of *Une saison en enfer* might well be considered to be the visual equivalent of the thrust towards the ambivalent, and more specifically towards the enantiosemic, which I have just described. (An enantioseme is a word which simultaneously means something and its opposite, e.g. *to cleave*, both 'to split apart' and 'to cling together'.) In recent years, Steve Murphy has been especially active, in a remarkable series of books, in presenting the links between Rimbaud's early poetry and the popular art of caricature towards the end of the Second Empire. His analyses have thrown light on many a reference which the passing of time has obscured. But one feature of the caricatural tradition which embodies both wit and obscurity in its very nature has been left aside. It is characterised not so much by the well known 'images d'Épinal' as by the 'devinettes d'Épinal', in which heads or features of humans or animals are hidden within the penny-plain or tuppence-coloured drawings. Sometimes it is a matter of simply inverting a head to see an alternative head; often the features are formed from those representing in the principal picture some part of a person's body, of a tree or whatever. There is the celebrated instance of facing silhouettes of heads both formed by and forming the outline of an ornate chalice; and we are now familiar with holograms which, from a slightly different angle of vision, change from one image to another, even, in some instances, producing the illusion of a three-dimensional object free-floating in space. It is the kind of thing which E.H. Gombrich investigates at the opening of *Art and Illusion* when he considers the nature of the switch which takes place in the mind when a drawing which can be interpreted as either rabbit or duck is seen first as one and then as the other: it is virtually impossible to register both simultaneously, even though the memory of one figure will be carried over to our direct experience of the other. Yet it is with this psychological conundrum that Rimbaud invites his readers to engage.

As early as 1893, in *La Plume*, the name of Rimbaud was associated with the English word 'rainbow': 'Rimbaud, comme son nom l'indique (rain-bow), est un arc-en-ciel, mais un arc-en-ciel de lune, et déployé par une nuit d'éclipse.' [Rimbaud, as his name (rain-bow) indicates, is a rainbow, but a rainbow caused by the moon, and displayed on the night of an eclipse.] More than one critic since has played with the arbitrary association to express the gamut of Rimbaud's moods and moments. To coincide with the

centenary of Rimbaud's death, a romp of a novel set exactly a
century after him, in 1991, is called *Rainbow pour Rimbaud*,
faithful in many ways to the poet's iconoclasm but informed less
by Karl Marx than by Groucho. Yet in the end, and although I
have in my turn been tempted by its alliteration into retaining it
for my title, I should like to propose a different visual image for
Rimbaud's vision.

The metaphor of the stroboscope seems far more apt than that
of the rainbow or even of the hologram to characterise Rimbaud's
writing and mental set and to suggest an appropriate strategy for
reading his work. It suggests dynamism as well as ambiguity. With
it, the physicist can follow movements too fast for the naked eye.
We are familiar with wheels apparently revolving slowly back-
wards on a cinema screen whereas we know that in fact they are
speeding forwards. It is all a matter of the relationship between
the speed of the shutter and the speed of the turning object. The
psychiatrist uses the stroboscope to provoke a crisis in a patient,
something those too old for discotheques will no doubt see as
similar to the effect of strobe lighting on a mass of young people
dancing. The theatre director switches it on briefly to transform
continuous human gestures into the staccato movements of seem-
ing puppets. We see the discontinuity while remaining aware of
the underlying continuity.

'Marine', one of the two free-verse poems collected in
Illuminations, offers a striking illustration of the stroboscopic
metaphor, ending on the phrase 'tourbillons de lumière' which
seems almost to be straight translation of the Greek roots of 'stro-
boscope': *strobos* and *skopein*. The whole poem shuttles between
references to land and sea, each implicated in the other, first in
alternate lines and then by transferred epithets within the lines:

> Les chars d'argent et de cuivre —
> Les proues d'acier et d'argent —
> Battent l'écume, —
> Soulèvent les souches des ronces —

Les courants de la lande,
Et les ornières immenses du reflux,
Filent circulairement vers l'est,
Vers les piliers de la forêt, —
Vers les fûts de la jetée,
Dont l'angle est heurté par des
tourbillons de lumière.

[Chariots of silver and copper —
Prows of steel and silver —
Strike the foam, —
Lift up the stumps of brambles —
The currents of the plain,
And the immense ruts of the ebbtide,
· Run eastwards in a circle,
Towards the pillars of the forest, —
Towards the trunks of the jetty,
Whose corner is struck by
swirls of light.]

It is naturally even more complicated than it appears, since a
subsidiary meaning of what we primarily believe to be a land-
bound vehicle – *char* – turns out to be a sea-going vessel. Likewise,
les souches des ronces, principally 'bramble-stumps', hide a rare
meaning as 'the nests of rays'. Out of this swirl of a seascape, in
which land and sea are interactively fused more closely the more
one investigates, there emerges at the close only a dazzling whirl of
light. The stroboscopic flickering is finally supplanted by bril-
liance, discontinuity by continuity of a third kind, synthesising
the contraries between which the critical poetic action is played
out. That synthesis does not destroy or denature the preceding
components. It remains in tension with them and it is not
sufficient to fill the gaps with everyday logic: we must trust to what
Eliot called the logic of the imagination.

This is true of the many parodic poems to which Rimbaud

33

turned after his earliest exercises in pastiche. One has to cleave to the parodied text in order to grasp the cleaving impact of the parody. It is equally true of those poems in which an obscene current runs under a seemingly benign surface. It is as if two texts there follow parallel tracks, with pivotal words and phrases linking them like unnoticed sleepers. In *Illuminations,* such hide and seek is brought to a state of complex perfection. Elements of parody, obscenity and references to other dubious practices such as drug-taking which could not be treated openly are subordinated to the demands of a higher aesthetic purpose or rather incorporated into that purpose. Doubtless an impulse towards self-censorship folded such ingredients into the mixture, even if we cannot be sure that Rimbaud destined it for public consumption. However, the very title of the collection, taken in conjunction with the obscurity of the texts, invites the stroboscopic metaphor, which is, as it were, a metaphor of metaphor itself. It is why Rimbaud seems to lie at the very heart of the poetic act and of poetic art as we now understand them. The brilliance of the visions, coupled with the reference, through the English use of the word for which Verlaine vouches, to the stark primaries of medieval manuscripts, dazzles and blinds, shimmers and endures. The gravitational pull of the sun is exceeded only by that of black holes.

Mallarmé the Maestro

Mallarmé is such an obvious master of form, increasing his technical wizardry as his poetry developed, that, as in the case of Gerard Manley Hopkins, we show due respect and are readily persuaded that what he has to say is no less carefully considered and likely, in consequence, to reward our intellectual attention. Nor, in either case, are we disappointed. Each in his not dissimilar way asserts himself as high priest of poetry, relishing the rare word, delighting in intricate patterns of sound, stretching syntax to its limits of comprehensibility and sometimes beyond, but all this, for the most part, within the traditional patterns of verse. Admiration comes easily, whereas the case for Rimbaud's prose poems has to be argued and proven by equivalent attention being focused on texts which pointedly reject traditional verse forms and the assumptions and expectations they create in the reader's mind.

Yet in addition to the verse poems which form the familiar bulk of his output, Mallarmé created the experimental text of *Un coup de dés jamais n'abolira le hasard*, and although this was, from Mallarmé's point of view, an unsatisfactory and paltry spin-off from the *Grand Œuvre* (with its alchemical overtones) which he envisioned but never accomplished, from the absolute *Livre* which he saw as the finality of the world, its interest has proved exceptional for subsequent generations of poets. To fail in some overreaching ambition may represent a higher achievement than success achieved within narrow limits.

The very obviousness of the visual impact of *Un coup de dés* might lead us to separate it from the rest of Mallarmé's work. I believe that this would be unwise. However different in their appearance the sonnets, for example, may be, they show on analysis a preoccupation with form – with that creation of a necessity out of the arbitrary which I have characterised as Cratylian nostalgia – which goes beyond the usual technicalities of versification. The impulse seems to grow stronger. The octosyllabic sonnets stress their verticality more than do those in alexandrines by virtue of the shorter line adopted. The more frequent recurrence of rhymes in octosyllables (simply in the sense that they occur every eight syllables rather than every twelve) discharges Mallarmé to some degree from the need to insist on repetition at that point in the line and so frees him to weave his many-ply phonology into the complex syntactical texture of the line. Yet even in the longer line Mallarmé strives to engage with verticality by a particular emphasis on rhyme. That emphasis shows clearly in the celebrated 'Sonnet en x' where, in an extraordinary *tour de force*, the same sound is retained for both masculine and feminine rhymes (in —yx / —ixe and —ore / —or), a nonce-word ('ptyx') being created for the occasion since the French language was short, by one, of the number of masculine rhymes needed. The sustained interplay between back and front vowels is an intellectual and, as André Spire would fairly argue, a physical, muscular delight which engages the reader in the effort of understanding and interpretation.

The case of 'Le vierge, le vivace et le bel aujourd'hui...' [The virgin, perennial and lovely today...] (first published in 1885) is scarcely less extraordinary in that, while the choice of rhyming words presents fewer difficulties, a single assonance is maintained throughout the sonnet. If this were virtuosity for its own sake, Mallarmé would doubtless be relegated to the limbo occupied by the *Rhétoriqueurs*. That he is not nor is likely to be is a measure of his capacity to address through metaphor his reflection on the difficulty of artistic creativity. The poet capitalises on the chance that 'le cygne' and 'le signe' ['swan' and 'sign'] are homophones in French, a clear example of retrieving the necessary from the arbitrary. Yet the creation of what might be seen as a frame for his poem, principally by virtue of the insistent vowel chosen for his rhyming words but also by its introduction at key points in the opening and closing lines (with further concentration on the sound in the last line of the octave), suggests that he is alert to spatial considerations before the writing of *Un coup de dés*. To represent this figuratively impresses the argument on the memory:

> Le vierge, le vivace et le bel aujourd'hui
>
> ivre
givre
fui!
>
> lui
délivre
vivre
l'ennui.
>
> agonie
nie,
pris.
>
> assigne,
mépris
>
> Que vêt parmi l'exil inutile le Cygne.

The number of 'i' sounds within this framework is unusually high, and the words which carry them either important in themselves or placed in key positions: 'Va-t-il nous déchirer', 'oublié', 'glacier', 'Un cygne', 'Magnifique mais qui...', 'stérile hiver a resplendi', 'infligée', 'Il s'immobilise'. Both eye and ear are focused on the 'i' but in different and complementary ways, since a yod (as in 'vierge') will not sound but merely appear the same as an 'i', while the graphy 'y', different in appearance from 'i', is indistinguishable in sound. Such distinctions are important in poetry that can be read entirely silently or out loud, but remain relatively minor differences when both eye and ear can be imaginatively trained on the text on either occasion. The gap becomes unbridgeable only when a poem abandons the horizontal line in favour of other pictorial and spatial forms.

Before turning to consider *Un coup de dés,* I should mention another aspect of Cratylian nostalgia manifest in this sonnet. It has less to do with shape than with colour, or rather the lack of it. Unlike Rimbaud in his sonnet 'Voyelles', Mallarmé does not here attribute a specific colour to the letter 'I', but it is apparent that the tight back vowel is associated in his poem with the blank seizure of creative sterility represented by the swan trapped in the ice, white on white. How different Rimbaud's 'I rouge', characterised by features evoking bright red (or suggestively connected with it) in contradistinction to the whiteness reserved by him for the vowel E:

> E, candeur des vapeurs et des tentes,
> Lances des glaciers fiers, rois blancs, frissons d'ombelles;
> I, pourpres, sang craché, rire des lèvres belles
> Dans la colère ou les ivresses pénitentes.

> [E, whiteness of steam and tents,
> Lances of lofty glaciers, white kings, the shimmer of umbels;
> I, scarlet, blood spat out, the laughter of lovely lips
> In anger or penitent hangovers.]

Such colour association is at root as arbitrary as the linguistic sign itself, a fact underlined by the different colours linked to different vowels by these two poets, yet each is endeavouring to suggest a necessary relationship fashioned in his respective sonnet. The reader responds to such incontrovertible authority by momentarily suspending his disbelief in associative necessity just as, under the spell of a poet's craft, he willingly abandons himself, against all logic, to the general promptings of a belief in linguistic necessity.

Mallarmé's octosyllabic sonnets occupy, as he himself observes in his prefatory note of 1897 to *Un coup de dés,* about one third of the blank page: the rest is silence. Those margins allow for the expansion of the poem into the recesses of the unencumbered imagination. His new poem, he declares, merely scatters this third across the whiteness in 'subdivisions prismatiques de l'Idée' [prismatic subdivisions of the Idea] which allow each image to emerge and drown again as the precision of the poem dictates. Narrative is purposely avoided, but this comes as no surprise, being an extension of the practice of Mallarmé's mature verse rather than a change of direction. Nor does he relinquish his concern to present his poem as a musical score available for reading out loud, even if to our eyes such a preoccupation seems both a failure to recognise the predominantly spatial importance of the text and to oversimplify its nature. For Mallarmé restricts his reading notes to two suggestions: first, that volume should correspond to type-size; and second, that intonation should follow the position on the page. His capacity for understatement is nevertheless considerable, since he goes on to observe that while his text continues in the mainstream of poetic tradition, its presentation is sufficiently novel to open a few eyes. 'Reconnaissons aisément que la tentative participe, avec imprévu, de poursuites particulières et chères à notre temps, le vers libre et le poëme en prose.' [Let us recognise freely that the endeavour is related, but surprisingly, to particular undertakings of which this age is fond: *vers libre* and the prose poem.]

That Mallarmé was in fact fully aware of the revolutionary nature of his enterprise and of its primarily visual nature is amply recorded elsewhere and evidenced by the exceptional care he took in preparing the pages for a publication of the text in book form which would never be realised. Furthermore, in a letter to André Gide on *Un coup de dés*, he linked the essentially musical notion of rhythm to its spatial representation. It is a magisterial reaffirmation of the principle of re-enactment, valid for this poem but of more general import: 'le rythme d'une phrase au sujet d'un acte, ou même d'un objet, n'a de sens que s'il les imite, et figuré sur le papier, repris par la lettre à l'estampe originelle, n'en sait rendre, malgré tout, quelque chose.' [The rhythm of a sentence concerning an act, or even an object, has no meaning unless it imitates it, and, figuring it on the paper, picked up by the letter from the original design, manages, in spite of it all, to capture something of it.] Paul Valéry, privileged to see the manuscript of the poem before its first publication, had his attention drawn to its layout and records his admiration: 'Il me sembla de voir la figure d'une pensée, pour la première fois placée dans notre espace... Ici, véritablement, l'étendue parlait, songeait, enfantait des formes temporelles... Il a essayé, pensai-je, *d'élever enfin une page à la puissance du ciel étoilé.*' [I had the impression of seeing the figure of a thought, placed in our space for the first time... Here, in very truth, space spoke, dreamed, gave birth to temporal forms... He has endeavoured, I thought, *to raise a page at last to the power of the starry sky.*]

There is a period affinity linking Wagner's concept of the *Gesamtkunstwerk*, Pater's idea of the arts all aspiring to the condition of music, and Mallarmé's endeavour to elaborate a text fusing elements spatial and musical, as well as verbal. Indeed the notion of recurrent leitmotiv may readily be applied to *Un coup de dés.* As well as semantic, they are typographical and dispositional, and even if all existing publications of the text are only approximations to Mallarmé's intentions (Mitsou Ronat's edition doubtless being the closest), they are adequately discernible for present purposes in most modern versions.

The dislocation of the page, through typographical variety and spatial disposition, represents a disruption of rational discourse, 'a raid on the inarticulate' which makes the inarticulate manifest in synchromesh with the articulate, a visual equivalent to the complex imbrications of Mallarmé's stutteringly parenthetical syntax. Yet spatial disposition and typographical variety also make such interrupted discourse susceptible to the establishment of a hierarchy. Each double page is thus carefully composed – as both design and score. Each word or group of words is placed for particular effect and presented in one of the eleven varieties of type, six roman and five italic, which interact with each other within a single opening (though never all at once, indeed to a maximum of six) and create chains of similar link-size across the total text. The most obvious concatenation is the reiterated title divided across much of the poem yet helping to bind it together. Roman or italicised capitals of smaller size weave strands among the components of the poem's major proposition, and among them again play lower-case elements of relatively lesser consequence. The linear is not totally abandoned, but considerations of the vertical and diagonal are inseparable from the horizontal, the word interacting powerfully with the page.

It is apparent, for example, that Mallarmé has moved beyond the pictograms or traditional *technopaignia* such as are found in the Greek Anthology, Stephen Hawes, Rabelais, George Herbert, or Lewis Carroll. Yet there are pictographic elements in his text re-enacting either details – such as the 'plume solitaire éperdue' floating alone, high on its almost empty page – or the broader narrative elements in the vision of a vessel sinking, embodied in the downward diagonal thrust of the typography – from top left to bottom right – in so many of the openings. The poem is not pure pictogram, however, even if several of its components are broadly pictographic, for it responds not so much to visualised objects for their own sake as to complex ideas represented rather by a diagrammatic, symbolic form than by a representational one. It is therefore primarily ideographic. These terminological distinctions, drawn from usage in respect of various Oriental languages, will be of particular value when we turn to Apollinaire. But they are useful here since they serve to underline the complexity of Mallarmé's undertaking, marrying as it does the pictographic and the ideographic in a projection which takes account of both reason and reverie. The unformulated blank page is an emblem of that chance which Mallarmé explores in the poem's formulations, a symbol of the unconscious on which words are endeavouring to inscribe their order. The poem enacts the never-ending struggle between potentiality and potency. As David Scott has written: 'In spite of the uneasy tension between the two, the relationship between visual and textual is essentially symbiotic: no expression of human experience would be complete without the involvement of both elements.'

That Mallarmé should ever have encouraged Odilon Redon to illustrate with lithographs such a self-illustrative text is paradoxical, even if they were considered, as has been suggested, to have a merely decorative function. His collaboration with Manet for an edition of his translation of Edgar Allan Poe's 'The Raven', published in 1875, and the emergence in the 1890s of *livres d'artiste* as a style of book production in its own right, might have led him to think of a new development along these lines. Certainly such productions for bibliophiles have been a feature of French publishing for the last hundred years and play a not insignificant role in the manifold interactions between poets and artists. It is not an aspect of the relationship between verbal and visual on which I intend to dwell, but neither is it negligible. Indeed it is one of the more obvious manifestations of that relationship and might be considered a natural outgrowth, given the availability of technical advances, from the preoccupations which we have been discussing.

Mallarmé ends his preface to *Un coup de dés* by reiterating his esteem for traditional versification. He may be said to represent, in both his practice and his theory, the point of reunion between the two dynamic types of reaction against the sterility of French verse which had started on their separate courses over sixty years before. One had revitalised versification from within and culminated in Mallarmé's intricate verse. The other, more radical, had firstly, with the prose poem, determined on a total rejection of verse and then, with *vers libres*, settled on the elimination of rhyme (or in some cases, such as Laforgue, on the retention of some rhyme but with irregular line-length). That such a point of juncture should occur in one master practitioner at the end of the nineteenth century provides a firm platform for exploring the developments of the twentieth. Mallarmé's early involvement with the *livre d'artiste* further denotes a particular facet of his work which reinforces his importance not just intrinsically but also as a harbinger of much to come.

42

Forms of Freedom

The search for compromise positions between traditional verse and the *poème en prose* led to various experiments with form in which, despite the epithet 'free', what in fact was sought were alternative forms of constraint. As my account has reached the threshold of the twentieth century, it is worth taking stock of what it has, perhaps surprisingly for an English reader, left out. Corbière and Laforgue bulk large, for example, in the history of French poetry as written by Eliot. The equally if not more important Lautréamont has no place in it. Yet from the formal point of view he and Laforgue are far more innovative than Corbière, who focused his inventiveness on variety of linguistic register. Of Lautréamont, for example, the poet Jacques Roubaud has pertinently written: 'les *Poésies* de Ducasse posent l'*abolition* du vers et la transformation définitive de poésie/prose, vers/non-vers en poésie/non-poésie.' [Ducasse's *Poésies* presuppose the *abolition* of versification and the definitive transformation of poetry/prose, verse/non-verse into poetry/non-poetry.] It is only considerations of space and balance that have led me to exclude them from my selective account, more willingly because they have not in practice had a marked influence on twentieth-century French poets in matters of form. My choice of instances from this century's poetry is subject to even greater arbitrariness. Nor will my presentation be strictly chronological, since coherence in individual chapters will sometimes require a stylistic thread to be followed from one poet to another. But first it is worth reviewing the position at the turn of the century through the range of the three poets who seem to present a tripod on which the formal variety of subsequent practice is based: Valéry, Claudel and Apollinaire.

43

Of the three, Valéry is the most traditional in appearance, vying with Mallarmé in intellectuality and complexity of formal constraints. As his notebooks have revealed, the high polish on the carefully wrought stanzas of *Charmes* represents the still surface of a turmoil of reflection and experimentation in style. To the reader who knows only that collection, it comes as a surprise perhaps that, like Mallarmé, Valéry wrote prose poems and as even more of a surprise that occasionally he indulged, like Apollinaire, in pictograms. For most readers he not unreasonably represents the tradition of cool classicism, something which went out of favour with Dada and Surrealism and which had to wait for the pendulum of favour to swing back from 'automatic writing' for its merits to be rediscovered.

Claudel, more prepared to let his experimentation show in public, started with rhyming quatrains but moved rapidly to the prose poems of *Connaissance de l'Est* and to the unrhymed *versets* of his plays and of the *Cinq Grandes Odes*. If his prose-lytising Catholicism is sometimes hard to swallow (indigestible even for an ecumenical heathen like myself), it need not detract from our recognition of him as one of the great innovators of modern French poetic form. The term 'versets' is applied in French to the verses of the Bible, and Claudel acknowledged his debt in that direction but suggested further that he also drew on Pindar, the ancient Greek tragedians and late Shakespeare. He saw traditional versification as too strict a metronomic piano-teacher and sought muscular flexibility in the larger form.

If constraints are less apparent, they are none the less present and important. Writing of his play *Partage de midi* to a sympathetic critic seeking elucidation, Claudel spelt out certain factors governing the unit of the individual line. Each had to be an 'unité respiratoire' [a breath-unit], something essential for the actor concerned but applicable too to the reader of his verse, so setting even a short line apart from its neighbours. Each had also to be a sense unit and a 'musical' unit, the latter term presumably meaning an acceptable phonetic pattern, appropriate to the circumstances of meaning and effect desired. The criteria remain highly personal, and nothing is said of what seems to me a considerable contribution: the appropriateness of the overall form to the grand sweep of the content. In a play, consistency of characterisation and development of narrative impose their own constraints. In the *Cinq Grandes Odes*, the former is irrelevant and the latter reduced, the *argumentum* placed at the beginning of each ode except the first removing any element of discovery, doubt or surprise in respect of the subject-matter.

The large scale of the odes and the complexity of their shifting meanings and metaphors militates against having a clear overview of the appropriateness of their shape. Nor are they all equally independent of existing forms: 'Magnificat' shares a liturgical style with its ecclesiastical predecessors and 'La Muse qui est la Grâce' gestures towards the Greek ode through its stated subdivisions into strophes, antistrophes and epode. The originality of the other three is that their shape is determined more intrinsically than by reference to an existing literary form.

'Les Muses' has no *argumentum*, but a footnote to the title refers the reader to a Roman sarcophagus brought to the Louvre from its original position on the road to Ostia. Its sculptured relief depicts the nine muses and determines the essentially descriptive nature of Claudel's poem. It also determines its horizontality until the point where, in the final passage added after a lapse of time and propriety, Claudel evokes his shipboard romance (the same as is recalled in *Partage de midi*), in which horizontality becomes everywhere and nowhere, 'là où le sol même est lumière' [where the very earth is brilliant light]. Although there is something of a recognised hierarchy among the muses, they are represented in such a way, by juxtaposition, as to mimic their equality of height and importance on the sarcophagus. The dynamic pulse of the *versets* emphasises this horizontality and obscures the inequalities of space allocated to each muse, to the extent that one scarcely notices that Terpsichore, Mnemosyne (usually considered the mother of the muses rather than one of them), Thalia,

45

Clio and Polymnia are treated at some length; Melpomene and Erato only briefly; and Calliope, Euterpe and Urania not at all. More often than not, they are evoked as a group: 'Les Neuf Muses! aucune n'est de trop pour moi!' What is underlined is the joint participation of all the muses not simply in the poet's inspiration but more particularly in moderating his tendency to excess:

Ô mon âme impatiente, pareille à l'aigle sans art! comment ferions-nous pour ajuster aucun vers? à l'aigle qui ne sait pas faire son nid même?

Que mon vers ne soit rien d'esclave! mais tel que l'aigle marin qui s'est jeté sur un grand poisson,

Et l'on ne voit rien qu'un éclatant tourbillon d'ailes et l'éblouissement de l'écume!

Mais vous ne m'abandonnerez point, ô Muses modératrices.

[O my impatient soul, like the artless eagle! how shall we manage to arrange a single line of poetry? like the eagle which doesn't even know how to build its nest?

May my line have nothing slavish about it! but like the sea-eagle which has pounced on a huge fish,

And lets nothing be seen but a brilliant swirl of wings and the dazzle of foam!

But you will not abandon me, O moderating Muses.]

This all-encompassing enthusiasm (in its modern as well as its etymological sense of divine frenzy) plays an even more marked cosmic role in 'L'Esprit et l'eau': 'Où que je tourne la tête / j'envisage l'immense octave de la Création!' [Wherever I turn my head / I survey the immense octave of Creation!] Here, the dynamism explores the two elements of the title through an extensive variety of their manifestations and associations. As 'l'esprit' in French means both mind and spirit, Claudel can range widely through matters intellectual and spiritual, associating 'l'esprit' with the intangible forces of the 'souffle': air and breath, divine afflatus and stamina. As to water, it is found in the slightest 'postillon' as in the widest ocean. It is the interaction of 'l'esprit' and 'l'eau', in speech as well as in spindrift, that expresses most fully the poet's quest for totality. And local effects capitalise on the suppleness of the versification so as to create, for example, a compulsive crescendo of exponentially lengthening lines as in

Ni
Le marin, ni
Le poisson qu'un autre poisson à manger
Entraîne, mais la chose même et tout le tonneau et la veine vive,
Et l'eau même, et l'élément même, je joue, je resplendis! Je
partage la liberté de la mer omniprésente!

[Neither
The sailor, nor
The fish that another fish drags off
To eat, but the thing itself and the whole barrelful and the
living vein,
And the sea itself, and the element itself, I exult in play, I
shine forth! I share the freedom of the omnipresent sea!]

Such local effects are less marked in Claudel, however, than the general appositeness of form. If we find the same insistent rhythms stretching the reader's capacities in 'La Maison fermée', it is because the search for the divine is conducted there through the architectural metaphor of the Chinese house, turned inwards on itself. Its squareness acts as a foil to the spiral exploration of its interior just as the fixed orientation of our outward appearances must be complemented by a probing of our inner depths. The poem is a kind of *mandala*. But still the driving length of line, heedless of syllable count or any strict regularity, impels the investigation and expresses the evangelical zeal.

More controlled is the writing of Saint-John Perse, even if at first sight his *versets* resemble Claudel's. His prosody takes genuine account of the syllabic and metrical traditions whereas the gesture towards the latter made by Claudel in evoking the 'iambe fondamental' in his 'Réflexions et propositions sur le vers français' was more apparent than real. For in practice Claudel understood by the iamb not an unstressed syllable followed by a stressed one but a variable number of unstressed syllables followed by a stressed one. He may have wished to avoid the complex precision of Greek terminology applied inappropriately to French verse, but his very imprecision is inevitably suspect. Saint-John Perse made a virtue of not theorising about poetry but getting on with writing it, and in all his mature work it is clear that the principle of appropriate re-enactment is at work. He makes this abundantly clear in various statements gleaned from his correspondence and rare interviews, the most general formulation of the principle appearing in a letter of 1956 to the *Berkeley Review* :

La poésie française moderne [...] ne se croit poésie qu'à condition de s'intégrer elle-même, vivante, à son objet vivant; de s'y incorporer pleinement et s'y confondre même substantiellement, jusqu'à l'identité parfaite et l'unité entre le sujet et l'objet, entre le poète et le poème. Faisant plus que témoigner ou figurer, elle *devient* la chose même qu'elle «appréhende», qu'elle évoque ou suscite; faisant plus que mimer, elle *est*, finalement, cette chose elle-même, dans son mouvement et sa durée; elle la vit et «l'agit», unanimement, dans sa mesure propre et dans son rythme propre: largement et longuement, s'il s'agit de la mer ou du vent; étroitement et promptement s'il s'agit de l'éclair.

[Modern French poetry [...] believes itself to be poetry only if it is integrated as a living force into its living subject-matter, fully incorporated into it and fused with its very substance, to the point where there is perfect identity and unity between subject and object, poet and poem. Doing more than bearing witness or figuring, it *becomes* the very thing it 'apprehends', evokes or conjures up; doing more than imitating, it *is*, in the end, that thing itself, in its movement and duration; it lives it and 'animates' it, in absolute unanimity with it, in its own measure and rhythm: expansively in space and time if it is the sea or the wind; narrowly and promptly if it's a question of the lightning.]

That Saint-John Perse is here referring most directly to his own practice is amply confirmed by the similarity of the terms he uses about his own work in private letters (made public in his *Œuvres complètes*) addressed to Mrs Katherine Biddle and Luc-André Marcel. Yet he was only formulating what had long since been his practice and that, widely recognised, of his contemporaries.

As with Claudel, it is perhaps the sheer length of some of the poems that obscures the principle at work. Yet 'Exil' manifestly espouses the rhythms and counter-rhythms of the sea by which it is set, and Saint-John Perse noted, when he sent his manuscript to Archibald MacLeish for typing, that the lines were 'astreintes au rythme de la vague' [bound to the rhythms of waves]. Nevertheless, when the poet is speaking as it were in his own voice, there is a marked tendency for an arithmetical principle to be applied: lines are grouped by seven, a number favoured by the poet from an early stage (as in 'Récitation à l'éloge d'une Reine'); and elsewhere, when the voice of Poetry is heard, the *versets* are grouped by three, which would become the preferred pattern throughout 'Pluies'. Yet the climactic canto of each of these poems spills over such containing norms, all the more clearly because of the very existence of those norms. Claudel is all abundance; Saint-John Perse measures his effects more carefully. So in 'Pluies', as the storm gathers, the *versets* lengthen until their bounds are broken by the cloudburst of canto VII, visibly darkening the page. As the rain subsides, so the lines shorten again and resume their triple grouping. And when the poem closes, the sun reappears and the recurring phrase, 'Seigneur terrible de mon rire', is dismembered on the dry threshold of the poem and *pavo*, the peacock emblematic of the sun, displays his iridescent tail to *pavor*, the fear brought by the rain, in a shimmer of vibrant plosives and voiced fricatives: '... Car telles sont vos délices, Seigneur, au seuil aride du poème, où mon rire épouvante les paons verts de la gloire.' [... For such is your delight, Lord, on the arid threshold of the poem, where my laughter frightens the green peacocks of fame.]

'Neiges' likewise espouses its subject-matter in its very form, blanketing the page as the snows blanket the earth, emblematic of absence and silence. After the opening canto has established the setting, each subsequent canto sets out in the imagination in a different direction, firstly westwards towards the Great Lakes and the Canadian border, then eastwards across the Atlantic towards France, and finally upstream in history towards the origins of language. The overall scheme is that of a clover-leaf pattern, each section returning to base before the new departure in the mind, having explored different stretches of whiteness on the way. And whereas the closing line of 'Exil' calls for a statement of identity, the *envoi* of 'Neiges' gestures towards silence.

Such careful control balanced against grand vision is typical of Saint-John Perse. It shows in the very detail of his verse-art, where traditional groupings of even numbers of syllables (with a marked preference for 6, 8 and 12) are enmeshed in units which, often by the insertion of an odd syllabic group or simply by the deft mixture of even groups, build into *versets* sharing little of Claudel's untamed *débordement*. The phonetic echoing is more apparent too in Saint-John Perse, the sense evolving through repetitions and sound-reversals in a dense texture which rewards close analysis. A particularly intense example may be found in canto III of 'Exil' where the voice of Poetry speaks through the poet:

«... Toujours il y eut cette clameur, toujours il y eut cette fureur,

Et ce très haut ressac au comble de l'accès, toujours, au faîte du désir, la même mouette sur son aile, la même mouette sur son aire, à tire-d'aile ralliant les stances de l'exil, et sur

toutes grèves de ce monde, du même souffle proférée, la
même plainte sans mesure
　À la poursuite, sur les sables, de mon âme numide...»

['Always there was this clamour, always there was this fury,
　And this very high backwash at the height of the tow,
always, at the pitch of desire, the same gull on its wing, the
same gull on its swing, sweeping swiftly together the stanzas of
exile, and on all the world's shores, uttered by the same
breath, the same measureless plaint
　Pursuing over the sands my Numidian soul...']

Too lengthy an analytical presentation of these lines would be
tedious, but a syllable count begins to show something of the
interplay of rhythmic components: 8, 8 / 6, 6, (2, 6), 8, 8, 8, 6, 9,
8, 8 / 8, 6. The bracketed 2+6 might be perceived as 8, echoing
the first line of this *laisse*, and indeed the 6+6 groupings might
be felt as an alexandrine or the 8+6 components as units of 14
syllables. Furthermore specialists might debate the role of the so-
called 'mute e' (better called 'e moyen' in recognition of its
ambivalent status) in this registration, but the broad principle
remains clear, and the intervention of the single odd number sets
off the very evenness of the others.

Because a metric principle as much as a syllabic one governs
this versification, number is the servant of vision rather than the
other way round. It is necessary to count Saint-John Perse's octo-
syllables and alexandrines only to observe how they are subsumed
in the larger prosodic pattern. Too traditionally tuned an ear will
single them out too much; too untrained an ear may well perceive
only mellifluous shapelessness. Saint-John Perse rejected the very
term 'prose poem' as misleading, preferring to consider all
unrhymed poems as 'poèmes non versifiés'. The attribute of poet-
ry is thereby brought to the fore. In his own practice, the syllabic
and metrical traditions are held in balance but are governed over-
all by the poet's shaping vision of his shifting subject.

51

That vision continues to shape the later poems. *Vents* and *Amers*, for example, evoke elemental forces on the earth and in man and, in their grand scale, are formal enactments of their subject-matter according to the same organic principle. More than one critic has objected to the baroque volutes of 'Amers' without recognising their appropriateness to the oceanic forces unleashed in the poem. But it is equally true that on such a large scale it is often hard to see the necessity of every detail: for that one must look to a more conventional lyric tradition which favours brevity.

Those whose style has been most influenced by Claudel and Saint-John Perse seem often to have been inspired by the grand vision rather than by the controlling techniques deployed in their verse. Léopold Sédar Senghor's 'L'Absente' includes direct quotation from Saint-John Perse as well as more general pastiche. His *Élégies majeures*, on the other hand, reduce the debt but in the process allow narrative and even anecdote to play a dominant role. In the work of Pierre Oster Soussouev, on the other hand, a careful and original balance is sought in his ample phrasing between number and metre, number in his case including poems in a numbered sequence, sometimes of exactly one hundred lines, sometimes rhyming in long-lined couplets, which themselves are governed in part by alliteration, though less systematically than in the ancient Anglo-Saxon tradition, as in this fragment from his 'Vingt-neuvième poème':

À présent
Que le désir devient destin, qu'à dessein il demande d'inscrire
Quelque flamme aux fenêtres, un tableau entier, d'un trait,
La terre intensément nous exauce, appesantit sur nous son
   étreinte,
Brûle, alimente un ferment. Des dieux, rocheux, ligneux,
   rugueux,
Affermissent notre alliance. Ils gardaient, inspectaient des îles
   mobiles.

[Now
That desire becomes destiny, that on purpose it asks to inscribe
Some flame on the windows, a whole picture, at a stroke,
The earth absolves us intensely, weighs its embrace heavily on us,
Burns and feeds a ferment. Gods, rocky, woody, rugged,
Affirm our alliance. They guarded, inspected mobile islands.]

Such a patient restatement of the continuum of the universe is
akin to Claudel's in spirit but infinitely more polished than his in
its detailed texture. Oster sees poetry as 'une machine à indiquer
l'univers' in which each line must be appropriate to its object and
adds with a note of regret: 'le poète atteint rarement à l'habileté
du boucher zen, opérant les yeux clos.' [a machine to indicate the
universe. ... The poet rarely achieves the deftness of the zen
butcher who operates with his eyes closed.]

The sense of absolute fitness of form to content, in which, as
Pierre Jean Jouve put it in his preface to *Sueur de sang*, 'la
recherche de la forme adéquate devient inséparable de la
recherche du fond', may well be a cornerstone of modern poetic
theory in France (at least among poets: self-engrossed criticism
seems to have been slow on the uptake) but it has such a variety of
possible manifestations that we should next look at the phenome-
non of Apollinaire's visual lyricism to see how different in prac-
tice is his expresion of the self-same principle.

53

Visual Lyricism

Apollinaire is undoubtedly the best known and the most obvious twentieth-century practitioner of that link between the verbal and the visual which expresses itself as pictogram or ideogram. The term on which he finally settled to cover both varieties (and also the rarer 'phonogram') was 'calligram', and *Calligrammes* is the title of the volume, written during the First World War and in the year immediately prior to it, which includes many of the most familiar examples.

Singularly susceptible to fashionable trends, Apollinaire also had a capacity for posturing which, in respect of his calligrams, led him to claim a spurious originality, a pioneering role on which others might improve: 'C'est un premier livre de cette sorte et rien ne s'oppose à ce que, d'autres allant plus loin dans la perfection que moi qui ai commencé cette sorte de poésie, il n'y ait des livres calligrammatiques fort beaux un jour'. [This is the first book of its kind, and nothing prevents other people going further this way towards perfection than I who began this kind of poetry, and one day producing beautiful calligrammatic books.] More to the point, in the same letter to his friend André Billy, is his typological insertion of calligrams in the recent development of poetic form: 'ils sont une idéalisation de la poésie vers-libriste et une précision typographique à l'époque où la typographie termine brillamment sa carrière, à l'aurore des moyens nouveaux de reproduction que sont le cinéma et le phonographe.' [They are an idealisation of vers-libre poetry and a form of typographical precision in an age when typography is ending its career brilliantly, at the dawn of the new means of reproduction represented by the cinema and the gramophone.]

54

It is true that the devising of picture-poems has always been sporadic rather than systematic. The third-century BC 'technopaignia' of Simmias, Dosiadas and Theocritus made familiar through the *Greek Anthology* can scarcely have escaped the attention of such an eclectic and voracious reader as Apollinaire. Over the centuries they had inspired the occasional foray into the bastard genre. Examples in Latin may be found from Porphyrius in the fourth century to Alcuin in the eighth. Stephen Hawes penned his 'Wings' in the fifteenth century. Puttenham's chapter on 'Proportion in Figure' in *The Arte of English Poesie* (1589) reminded practitioners of the availability of geometrical form for verse. In England, George Herbert, George Wither and, later, Lewis Carroll and Dylan Thomas among others, exploited the possibilities in various ways. In France, Rabelais's 'dive bouteille' stimulated a revival of interest, and Mellin de Saint-Gelais and Grisel in the sixteenth century, Angot de l'Éperonière in the seventeenth, and Pannard and Capelle in the eighteenth made their inconsequential contributions. Charles Nodier's *Le Roi de Bohême et ses sept châteaux* (1830) includes examples far more directly related to the tradition (such as pan-pipes in the manner of Theocritus' 'Syrinx') than Hugo's more often quoted near-contemporary poem 'Les Djinns'. The elongated lozenge form of the latter relates less to the meaning of the poem than do the many crosses drawn in words by earlier Christian didacticists in various countries. Yet it is clear that the very fixity of the mould into which words were being poured in such a tradition was analogous to that of existing verse forms. Why then should Apollinaire, who was so little systematic in anything, have set so much store by his revival of the practice?

The main thrust of an answer seems to lie in his interest in the visual arts and in the revolution in artistic expression which was taking place among his contemporaries and friends. In western art, Cubism was, after all, the first development to call into question the principles of perspective which had held sway since the Renaissance. Multiple points of view found simultaneous representation on the canvas, which thus challenged centuries of assumptions and brought duration into focus on a two-dimensional surface. Previously, painting had striven to indicate three dimensions, that of time being left to implicit interpretation. As the camera had usurped the brush as a tool for visual representation and record, painters sought to affirm their creativity in other ways. Where the Impressionists had concentrated on surface texture, leaving perspective to play a traditional role, the Cubists modified the basic structure.

However dimly and confusedly aware of this development Apollinaire was, he lent a willing ear to his painter-friends and relished the role of champion for their cause, aware as a journalist that publicity for a controversial avant-garde would be publicity for himself. He was undoubtedly sensitive to the radiant capacity of words not simply for their sense but also for their potential as shapes on the page. This is true of the shape of individual letters and of the varied shapes of words combined together to the point where the manuscript alone, not any typographically printed version, is a satisfactory index of the total effect. Rising to a challenge equivalent to that met by the Cubists and by the Simultaneism of Robert Delaunay, but paradoxically opposite to it given the different starting points of the media of paint and words, he seeks to counteract the duration of discourse by emphasising the two-dimensional, pictorial effect of words on the page. Most of the component parts of his calligrams are pictographic, that is to say they represent visually the object referred to or described in the words of which they are comprised. But they are rarely alone on the page, and in this regard differ from traditional technopaignia. Some novel interest may thus be generated by the combination of pictograms, juxtaposed in ways which might be seen as equivalent to the fragmentation of viewpoint in Cubist paintings or even anticipating the technique of arresting juxtapositions in Surrealist art.

Apollinaire was also aware, however, of different alphabets across the world, of hieroglyphs and ideograms, and the extra visual dimension which their concatenation deployed. The English reader does not need reminding of the importance Pound attached to Fenollosa's study of Chinese characters. A link can readily be seen between the latter's observation that 'in all poetry a word is like a sun, with its corona and chromosphere; words crowd upon words, and enwrap each other in their luminous envelopes until sentences become clear, continuous light-bands' and Saussure's remark about the generative units of language: 'un terme donné est comme le centre d'une constellation, le point où convergent d'autres coor-données dont la somme est indéfinissable' [a given term is like the centre of a constellation, the point on which converge other co-ordi-nates whose sum is indefinable]. Claudel was to characterise Chinese ideograms as synthetic, arguing that western graphies are by contrast analytical: 'L'idéogramme chinois est un être, la lettre occidentale est surtout un acte, un geste, un mouvement' [The Chinese ideogram is a being, whereas the western letter is first and foremost an act, a gesture, a movement], but there is perhaps less difference that at first appears, a fact that Henri Michaux would subsequently explore and exploit in his own way.

It might be said that Apollinaire tried to turn the analytic into the synthetic by attempting to fuse visual and verbal components. In the process, much is inevitably sacrificed. Legibility can be a real problem. The crudeness of the designs sometimes leaves the reader nonplussed until he has deciphered the words which explain and legitimise the shape. Yet during that process, with its concentration on the meaning of the words, the image is lost from view. No reading out loud is possible without the pictorial element, crucial to the very nature of the hybrid, being aban-doned. Uncertain and uneasy visual rhythms endeavour to compensate for those of words in sequence. It is as difficult to take seriously as poetry the largely inconsequential statements which the patient reader deciphers as it is to pay more than fleeting attention to the diagrammatic images. The two compo-nent media have validity only in combination, yet our confidence is undermined by their separate poverty of interest.

Calligrams were not the only expression of Apollinaire's interest in a marriage of the visual and the verbal, however, even if they are its most striking manifestation. His explorations led him to incorporate pictographic elements within otherwise linear poems, as in 'La Petite Auto', '2ᵉ canonnier conducteur' or 'Du coton dans les oreilles'. He is generally most successful, indeed, when he allows his sensitivity to the visual and pictorial to embody itself in words in ways that bring him more into the mainstream of the phenomenon we have been investigating. The exceptional use of italics for the opening poem of *Calligrammes*, 'Liens', is significant in a collection in which the eye is so insistently invited to interrupt its function as a scanner of sense. The cursive typeface, seemingly dynamic and yet, if psychologists of perception are to be believed, tending to slow the reading eye, seems to underline the significance of the title-word as a metaphor of metaphor. Communication is all in an age when the technological development of all forms of communication was so readily apparent in car and aeroplane, cinema, telephone and radio. It prepares us for the often abrupt juxtapositions of such a very painterly poem as 'Les Fenêtres' which invites us to travel the world of light, shape and colour, with the interruptions of punctuation abandoned and word-play intervening as it were to re-enact the flights of fancy which connect the spatial references:

Du rouge au vert tout le jaune se meurt
Quand chantent les aras dans les forêts natales
Abatis de pihis
Il y a un poème à faire sur l'oiseau qui n'a qu'une aile
Nous l'enverrons en message téléphonique

[From red to green all yellow dies
When macaws sing in their native forests
Chopped one-winged birds
There is a poem to be written on the bird which has only one wing
We shall send it as a telephone message]

A pictographic impulse is contained within the horizontal play-
fulness of subsequent lines:

> Tours
> Les Tours ce sont les rues
> Puits
> Puits ce sont les places
> Puits
>
> [Towers
> The towers are streets
> Wells
> Wells are squares
> Wells]

A kind of phonogram is incorporated in 'l'oie oua-oua trompette
au nord' [the wawa goose goes trumpeting to the north] and the
poem, still enacting its leaps through a ripple of puns, ends with
a summary of its own programme of exploration of the universe
of travel and the world of aesthetic metaphor:

> Du rouge au vert tout le jaune se meurt
> Paris Vancouver Hyères Maintenon New-York et les Antilles
> La fenêtre s'ouvre comme une orange
> Le beau fruit de la lumière
>
> [From red to green all yellow dies
> Paris dull Vancouver yesterday Hyères now Maintenon
> New York and the Windy Indies
> The window opens like an orange
> Light's luscious fruit]

Whatever one might think of such playful pyrotechnics, there
is little doubt that a calligrammatic awareness is a legitimate form
of expression for Cratylian nostalgia. When it assumes a readable

form, it comes very close to those shaping forces which we have seen governing poems of the highest and most serious ambition. It is used to excellent effect, for example, in 'Océan de terre' which closes the section 'Lueurs des tirs' in which the pervasive mud of the war zone assumes cosmic proportions. The very circumstances lead to the earth suffering a sea-change while remaining recognisably earth (leaving us less uncertain about vehicle and tenor of the metaphor than we are in Rimbaud's 'Marine'). In devising such a shelter as he may, the poet imagines an ark for his survival. Within the long unrhymed lines of the beginning and end of the text, Apollnaire inserts the following brief construction:

> Maison humide
> Maison ardente
> Saison rapide
> Saison qui chante
> Les avions pondent des œufs
> Attention on va jeter l'ancre

> [Damp house
> Burning house
> Quick season
> Singing season
> The aeroplanes lay eggs
> Watch out for the anchor being thrown]

It is indeed a literal image of Noah's Ark floating on the rising tide of mud envisioned as an ocean full of tentacular threats, 'poulpes' [octopus] being named four times in the eighteen-line poem, their menacing 'bec' [beak] twice, and the jet of their self-preserving ink equated ambiguously to that of the poet. The rapidly recurring rhymes signal a difference from what has preceded; and the anchor is placed where the anchor would be, showing below the hawse-hole of the solitary apostrophe.

Such a thoroughly assimilated pictographic impulse is not what Apollinaire is most remembered for, which tends to shuttle uneasily between the poles 'de la tradition et de l'invention / De l'Ordre et de l'Aventure' [of tradition and invention / of Order and Adventure] to which he himself drew attention. On the one hand, his traditional lyricism lulls, while on the other he jolts with the shock of the ostensibly new. His very inconsistency of approach may be seen as a virtue or a limitation, yet there is little doubt that his poetry is engaged in the quest which uses the visual as a stimulus for a reconsideration of how best to shape the verbal. His provisional title for an early group of calligrams was 'Et moi aussi je suis peintre'[I too am a painter], and he showed himself aware of the major challenge that painting could throw down to poetry: 'dans la peinture tout se présente à la fois, ... dans la littérature, dans la musique, tout se succède et l'on ne peut revenir sur tel mot, sur tel son au hasard' [in painting everything shows itself simultaneously, ... in literature and music, everything is successive and you can't backtrack on a given word or sound as you please]. Grappling with simultaneity led him perhaps to too narrow a vision of how to attain it, focusing on immediacy rather than on the final effect for the reader. But whenever he assimilated his material and forgot his posturing, he showed himself no less capable of achieving new and appropriate forms according to the same principle, however different the expression, than did the other poets of his age that we have been investigating.

Space Exploration

L ettrism, Spatialism, and the international phenomenon of
concrete poetry all owe Apollinaire a debt, though seem-
ingly to the most meretricious – or at least the most *appar-
ent* – aspect of his work. Each movement developed its own
emphases and encouraged its practitioners to explore the rela-
tionship between the visual and verbal in the literal shaping of the
text on the page. Many individual poets before them and indepen-
dently of them, however, have recognised the interest of creating
significant voids and investigating ways in which unorthodox
typographical presentation might, without going beyond the
limits of language (as some concrete poetry was to do), tap some
lyrical source and focus attention on the refreshment it might
bring.

Already in 1913, Cendrars had published his *Prose du
Transsibérien et de la petite Jehanne de France*, illustrated by
Sonia Delaunay, a concertina in which variety of typeface and an
irregular spatial disposition were joined by a swirling riot of
colour. Advances in printing technology made it increasingly
possible to envisage such developments, even if high costs were an
inhibition for some. The adherents of Dada, intent on breaking
the mould of conventional attitudes in art and society, often
expressed their anarchic radicalism by beating and breaking the
bounds between the verbal and the visual. Word-play was to the
fore. In conjunction with line-breaks, additional spacing to
replace traditional punctuation was used for example in Francis
Picabia's 'Délicieux', which first appeared in the July 1917 issue
of *391*, to highlight particular words, question fixed formulations
and generally disrupt lazy reading habits:

SPACE EXPLORATION

Étant tous deux
 décousus
au jour   le jour
 plus seul que partout
  pour terminer quelquefois
   le bout du nez
dans ma vie
 authentique
s'il est possible
 la nécessité matérielle
  je suis sûr apporte
   la bonne chance

«Cette époque n'est qu'une femme malade—
laissez-la crier, tempêter, disputer,
laissez-lui briser table et assiettes.»

                «—Es-tu fragile?
                Garde-toi des mains de l'enfant!
                L'enfant ne peut vivre,
                S'il ne casse quelque chose…»

[Both of us being
 disjointed
from hand   to mouth
 lonelier than anywhere
  finishing up sometimes
   at the tip of my nose
in my life
 authentic
if it's possible
material necessity
  I am sure brings
   good luck

63

'This age is nothing but a sick woman —
let her argue rant and rail
let her smash table and plates.'

> *'— Are you fragile?*
> *Beware the hands of the child!*
> *The child cannot live*
> *Without breaking something...'*]

The dislocations, including the change of typeface to register a change of mood and moment, and even the final restoration of initial capitals, contribute to an appropriately disruptive expression of a domestic row without sacrificing reflection on lessons learned from the experience. The patterned blocking and stepped effect of increasing indentation are as much part of a visual collage as the unpunctuated juxtapositions of the opening stanza are of a verbal one. The presentation in all its aspects contributes to a mental image created as much by the reader as by the text. As Jacques Roubaud has observed in *Dire la poésie*, himself inserting telling blanks into his prose, and paying passing homage to Mallarmé's 'absente de tous bouquets' [(flower) absent from all bouquets] and its associated idea 'suggérer, voilà le rêve' [to suggest, that is the ideal]:

Le poème dans le livre n'est pas une notation, une partition de la voix; les silences de la voix ne sont pas des traductions des blancs de la ligne; l'une et l'autre lecture construisent, imaginaire, un *double*, qui est cette poésie, absente de chaque poème, s'il est entendu et lu, mais plutôt se situe derrière chacun, un peu derrière chacun, à l'écart oblique et qui derrière chacun vous regarde.

[The poem in the book is not a notation, a score for the voice; the voice's silences are not translations of the blanks in the lines; both kinds of reading construct an imaginary *double*, which is the poetry, absent from each poem when heard and read, but situated rather behind each one, a little behind each one, well away slanting and which from behind each one peers out at you.]

Even exaggerated concentration on phonology, such as one finds in Robert Desnos's 'Élégant cantique de Salomé Salomon' [Elegant Hymn for Salome Solomon], from *L'Aumonyme* (1923), with its untranslatable insistence, turn and turn about, on m and n, funnels our attention visually on those letters at the end while still allowing – in the original at least – their homonymic echoes to reverberate:

> Mon mal meurt mais mes mains miment
> Nœuds, nerfs non anneaux. Nul nord
> Même amour mol? mames, mord
> Nus nénés nonne ni Nine.
>
> Où est Ninive sur la mappemonde?
>
> Ma mer, m'amis, me murmure:
> «nos nils noient nos nuits nées neiges».
> Meurt momie! môme: âme au mur.
> Néant nié nom ni nerf n'ai-je!
>
> > Aime haine
> > Et n'aime
> > haine aime
> > aimai ne
> >
> > M N
> > N M
> > N M
> > M N

65

[Mourning my malady my hands mime
Knots, nerves not rings. No north nor
Malleable amours? mouth mammaries
Naked nipples nun nor Ninos.

Where is Nineveh on the map?

Maritime murmurs hum, my mates:
'our Niles drown our nights born as snow'.
Mourn the mummy! mite, frame your mind.
Nothingness denied I've neither name nor nerve!

　　　Love hate
　　　Only love
　　　hate love
　　　loved hate

　　　　M N
　　　　N M
　　　　N M
　　　　M N]

Such Fair Isle knitting with words bears the stamp of clever-
ness in the mould of the fifteenth- and sixteenth-century
Rhétoriqueurs and becomes, in a case such as this, an acrostic
conceit, casting doubt on the idea that poetry is what gets lost in
translation. Yet far simpler forms were entertained, such as
Benjamin Péret's readily translatable, fairytale line in 'Le Travail
anormal', first published in *Intentions* in 1924:

Le caniche grossit grossit grossit grossit
et s'habilla de couleurs claires.

[The poodle grew and grew and grew and grew
and dressed in bright colours.]

It is the very obviousness of such practices which limits their interest, yet by their very presence they alert us to an impulse which is susceptible of subtler exploration and expression. Michel Leiris plays engagingly with words when producing, for example, his 'Sceptre miroitant' [Shimmering sceptre] in which MOI [me] and ROI [king] are picked out among the interactive words MOURIR [die], AMOUR [love] and MIROIR [mirror] which form a kind of sceptre while figuring a setting of MUR [wall] and AIR which appear as fragmented decor:

When language draws attention to itself, it engages in a manner of self-publicity. Used as an integral component of the poetic thrust, it can act as a hidden persuader. Put to commercial ends, it strikes the eye and mind, becoming memorable in advertisements devised not just to capture our attention but also to open our wallets. There is a significant shift in sensibility between the ways hoardings were viewed by Mallarmé, as prosaic, and by Apollinaire, who wrote in 'Zone': 'Tu lis les prospectus les catalogues les affiches qui chantent tout haut / Voilà la poésie ce matin et pour la prose il y a les journaux' [You read the prospectuses catalogues and posters which sing out loud/That's this morning's poetry and for prose there are the newspapers]. Rimbaud's alertness to everyday popular art including advertisements (such as 'Enghien chez soi') makes him a forerunner of such a publicity page as Tristan Tzara composed for *391* in November 1920 to advertise a special sale of Dadaist publications (reproduced in Massin's superb *La Lettre et l'image*). Seen in its entirety, it is a typographer's nightmare, all the canons of order being overthrown, almost as disorientating as a page from a Japanese newspaper which requires reading in three different directions. Following the recommendations and practices of the Italian Futurists, typefaces are mixed in style and size, even within words or phrases, which can run vertically up or down the page or at an angle, or even upside down, sometimes being outlined by a rectangle, a square or a rhomboid. Digits and non-linguistic signs (arrows, exclamation marks, even the conventional star representing the *légion d'honneur*) add to the complexity. Provocation is the point; and it functions verbally as well as visually when the reader focuses more closely on what is printed. In addition to pastiches of small ads *mises en abyme* within the advertisement we find a splendid example of bad publicity being used as good publicity in a quotation attributed to Anatole France, a *bête noire* of Dada and Surrealism: 'Tzara est un idiot, son livre un attentat aux mœurs' [Tzara is an idiot, and his book an assault on decency].

It is not our purpose here to investigate the modes of advertising, however clever they may be, since they tend to exploit stereotypes rather than explore their passionate interstices. It must be recognised, however, that there is in this respect a gradation rather than a firm partition between poetry and posters. Equally, the decision as to whether a particular artefact should be classed as linguistic or pictorial is often a delicate one. When a single creative artist such as Henri Michaux produces a continuum spanning both media, the critical urge to classify is happily disarmed, yet there are cases of such multi-media artists who, like Arp, generally respected traditional categorisation.

In the 1940s, Isidore Isou elaborated the theories of Lettrism, of which Jean-Louis Curtay has been the admiring historian, and of which Pierre Albert-Birot was the most notable precursor. New signs were devised to complement or replace the alphabet in ways not dissimilar to those which Henri Michaux had explored in the 1920s. New words were forged, again reminiscent of Michaux or Robert Desnos or Michel Leiris, but applied with less dexterity and wit. Whereas for them such innovations were a means of liberating the imagination, they seem among the Lettrists to have had a constraining effect, limiting the range of expression and restricting the approach to form. The results are generally unpronounceable, unedifying, inglorious.

The movements of the 1960s have the merit of wit and often illustrate in a nutshell how form and meaning can come together in a partnership of inseparability. When 'ha k' is the sole word inscribed on a page and its missing 'w' poised high above the other letters as if ready to dive on its backswept wings, it is a conceit requiring that particular arrangement on the paper for its realisation. Just as no phoneme carries meaning of itself, but needs to be interpreted, within a phonetic pattern and according to its particular semantic context, so each letter is susceptible of overdetermination as a graphic unit. Here the w becomes the hovering hawk. Elsewhere a letter would become whatever the visual imagination sees in it, and so participate in a process as familiar to scribes bent on illuminating manuscripts as it is to print designers working at their computer screens. The result is inevitably slight if the technique is used alone, but one of Apollinaire's more legible calligrams, 'La Colombe poignardée et le jet d'eau', exploits two capital letters, printed in large bold type, as an integral part of the design: the C becomes the marking on the collar-dove's throat and the O the mouth of the pipe from which the fountain gushes. Such features are subsumed, however, within the overall pattern, in which traditional symbolism (the dove of peace, the fountain of life) participates to an important degree in an evocation of friends dispersed by warfare and threatened by death.

69

The *poésie éclatée* of André du Bouchet, Philippe Denis and others works on the basis of a principle which Leiris states in *Biffures* as 'faire comuniquer entre eux les différents îlots jetés sur le blanc du papier' [having the different islands thrown on to the white paper communicate between one another]. Pierre Torreilles in his turn uses large sheets of paper in landscape mode to create visually appealing manuscripts where the fall of a comma, sometimes detached from words, emphasises the spatial reading to which he invites us. The absent links allow room for the imagination to invest its efforts, charging the unsaid with meanings which can develop differently with each new reading. Georges Perec's wittily provocative *Espèces d'espaces* of 1974 prompts reflection on our exploration of space even by writing at a steeply oblique angle down the page the word 'horizontale' in the sentence 'une ligne assez strictement horizontale se dépose sur la feuille blanche'. This scarcely goes beyond the *boutade*. But let a single page from du Bouchet's 'Aveuglement, peinture' (*Une tache*, 1988) show the extraordinarily complex interactions involved at a deep level of serious sensitivity:

tout support sera figure déjà.　　*futur*
　　　　　　　　　　　　　　　　　comme fraîcheur

　　　　　　　　　　　　　　　　　comme
　　　　　　　　　　　　　　　　　fraîchir sur ce qui
«peindre contre la peinture».　　*ayant déposé,*
　　　　　　　　　　　　　　　　　brûle encore.

　　　　　　　　　　　　　　　　　elle-même la source
　　　　　　　　　　　　　　　　　se déplace.

　　　　　　　　　　　　figure　　*ne pas être arrêté*
de la face soustraite, la mienne aussi peut-être　*par ce qui*
　　— et par les yeux, lorsque je vois.　*se sera localisé,*
　　　　　　　　　　　　　　　　　attenant à un vide
　　　　　　　　　　　　　　　　　— à ce qui,
　　　　　　　　　　　　　　　　　inoccupé,
　　　　　　　　　　　　　　　　　et
　　　　　　　　　　　　　　　　　pour avoir été
　　　　　　　　　　　　　　　　　occupé un jour,
　　　　　　　　　　pour une part　*en retour passera*

SPACE EXPLORATION

seulement: ce n'est que le fond du contenant une fois
encore rapporté à sa face qui n'est pas
la mienne uniquement.

aujourd'hui
momentanément
pour le vide.

existence part.

comme
futur se fait,
existence part.

il arrivera qu'on bute – chacun – sur sa
disparition : c'est le support : il éclaire.

[every medium is already an image.

future
as coolness

as
cooling on what
having settled,
still burns.

'paint against painting'.

the source itself
changes place.

image
of the subtracted face, mine too perhaps
— and by the eyes, when I can see.

not to be stopped
by what
has been confined,
reaching a void
— reaching what,
unoccupied,
and
for having been
occupied one day,
in return will pass
today
momentarily
for the void.

for one part
only : it is merely the bottom of the container once
again brought back to its face which is not
mine alone.

existence departs.

as
future becomes,
so existence departs.

we shall all happen to stumble – each one of us – on our
disappearance : it is the medium : it enlightens.]

One last instance of such writing which, unlike pictograms, can
be read out loud without the total loss of the graphic effect, but

which needs to treated when read almost as a musical score, is the following poem drawn from Lorand Gaspar's superb 1972 collection, *Sol absolu*, here in its 1982, revised form, in which the poet introduces a comment on the interplay between medium and message in the word 'dess(e)in'.

d é s e r t

  ce qui reste de musique
  quand le dess(e)in n'est plus visible
  comme si la lumière avait érodé
  le temps et le lieu qui sont aux choses
  comme si la grammaire des fonds était lisible
  à la main qui s'éclaire sur les regs

a n a c h o r è t e s

  lézards

   s e r p e n t s

    hyènes et cynhyènes

  par les gorges du matin
  sur les pentes du soir

les routes non tracées du mouvement solidaire

  l'oryx sauvage
  la gazelle d'Arabie

le vent sur les plaines du Sam au sud de l'Euphrate

  plantes à soude
  arbustes rabougris
  plateaux gréseux
  psammites taillés à pic
  thalwegs de ruissellement
  fonds de mer éocène

SPACE EXPLORATION

la   même   nudité   de   la   vie

une seule

r   e   s   p   i   r   a   t   i   o   n

[d e s e r t

    whatever music remains
    when the design is no longer visible
    as if the light had eroded
    the time and place inherent in things
    as if the grammar of the depths were readable
    in the hand which brightens over the dunes

a n c h o r i t e s

    lizards

      s n a k e s

        hyenas and jackals

    through the gorges of the evening
    on the slopes of the morning

the untraced routes of collective movement

    the wild oryx
    the Arabian gazelle

the wind over the Sam plains south of the Euphrates

    soda plants
    stunted shrubs
    sandstone plateaux
    sheer psammites
    streaming thalwegs
    eocene seabeds

the   same   nakedness   of   life

a single

r   e   s   p   i   r   a   t   i   o   n]

The instigator of Spatialism, Pierre Garnier, endeavours in various ways to include such additional dimensions in his work, but essentially Spatialism is a French branch of concrete poetry and acknowledges itself as such by its international links, notably with German and Japanese writers, and in the very title of its manifesto: *Spatialisme et poésie concrète.* Garnier has a penchant for using signs available on the typewriter keyboard beyond the alphabet: horizontal and oblique strokes, parentheses, punctuation of various sorts often used independently of words. The proportion of blank paper to print is generally far higher than is usual (and far higher than in Lettrism), especially where there is a purposeful evocation of space, as in *Le Jardin japonais, Tristan et Iseult* or *Congo: poème pygmée.* We need to backtrack to some ostensibly more conventional writers to find a balance which exploits the traditional craft of poetry while remaining sensitive to the possibilities of spatial form.

Sign and Line

In *Ceci n'est pas une pipe*, Michel Foucault writes: 'Signe, la lettre permet de fixer les mots; ligne, elle permet de figurer la chose. Ainsi, le calligramme prétend-il effacer ludiquement les plus vieilles oppositions de notre civilisation alphabétique: montrer et nommer; figurer et dire; reproduire et articuler; imiter et signifier; regarder et lire.' [As a sign, the letter allows words to be fixed; as a line, it allows the thing to be figured. So the calligram claims to erase by its playfulness the oldest oppositions of our civilisation of the alphabet: showing and naming, figuring and saying; reproducing and articulating; imitating and signifying; looking and reading.] The shift away from fixed forms of verse has allowed the development of different kinds of spatial shaping, and with it has come the realisation that traditional verse can in fact accommodate elements of spatial awareness. We have seen how it can apply to the Mallarmé of the sonnets. If his foregrounding there of the phonetic contributes to the appearance of necessity created out of the largely arbitrary conventions of language, it acts as a reminder that hypotyposis (or imitative harmony) can legitimately be made to participate in the poem's broader purposes and be converted in sophisticated hands from the linear to the spatial.

With almost mathematical precision, Valéry places the word 'temple' in 'La Jeune Parque' in such ways as to trace a parallelogram which not only gives the outline of the metaphorical poetic 'temple' he is constructing but overdetermines the production of its shape by incorporating a specialised meaning of the word: 'template'. In his fascinating book *Mimologiques: voyage en Cratylie*, Gérard Genette notes Valéry's scepticism of imitative harmony and asks 'que peut être au juste une *harmonie non imitative?*' [What exactly can *non-imitative harmony* be?]. Because he asks the wrong question, he inevitably reaches the unacceptable conclusion that Valéry's poetics meets a dead end and embodies an irreducible contradiction between formalism on the one hand and 'l'indissolubilité du son et du sens' on the other. The more fruitful question would have been to retain the word 'imitative' but change the word 'harmonie' to 'mise en forme', thus allowing the incorporation of sound patterns but not being restricted to them. But since his work deals essentially with the phonic aspects of words, Genette generalises to all modern poetry the unresolved paradox which he perceives in Valéry: 'La contradiction y reste irrésolue, entre un très vif parti pris formaliste et conventionaliste, et une sorte de réflexe héréditaire de valorisation de la mimésis. Cette contradiction est encore aujourd'hui [1976] au cœur de toutes les poétiques «modernes».' [The contradiction remains unresolved in him between an extreme commitment to conventional formalism and a kind of hereditary reflex which throws mimesis into relief. This contradiction still lies today [1976] at the heart of every 'modern' poetics.] It is inherent in my argument that our interpretation of mimesis needs to be extended to include spatial factors of representation and that it is a distortion and restriction of Aristotle not to do so.

In discussing Apollinaire, we saw how the confrontation of the duration-bound arts of the word with the two dimensions of the fine arts led to responses which rose in various ways and with varying degrees of success to that challenge. In many respects, the more rewarding response to it, as far as twentieth-century writing is concerned, has involved an acknowledgement of the *silence* of the visual arts. Articulated language presupposes sound even when the process of reading involves only eye and mind. Certainly, many other factors have predisposed writers to an investigation of silence, notably the philosophies of nothingness and the void. But such was also true of Bergson's investigation into time and duration which so influenced Apollinaire, Proust

76

and others. To highlight the interaction between different modes of perception and expression is not to deny the importance of other circumstantial considerations, especially when they influence a whole generation of thinking.

Pierre Reverdy shows intense interest in the visual arts and has, even more legitimately than Apollinaire, been dubbed a 'Cubist' poet. His writings on art, gathered under the title *Note éternelle du présent*, embody an awareness of the interaction of time and timelessness which that title encapsulates. His largely Hegelian views on beauty, pitching the work of art higher than anything produced in nature, mean that he can apply to poetry as well as to painting the principle that emotion must be distilled from feelings, and qualities of mind and spirit from anecdote. Such a non-imitative view of art means that he can envisage, as Andrew Rothwell puts it in his fine study, *Textual Spaces: the poetry of Pierre Reverdy*, 'a higher form of mimesis where the work of art mirrors essential, rather than contingent, aspects of reality'. Rothwell adds later: 'It is on this abstract level of intention, and in the manipulation of the signifying systems of poetry (vocabulary, syntax, typography, rhythm, rhyme, metaphor) to create an anti-mimetic descriptive form based on the controlled use of ambiguity, that the real analogies with cubist painting lie.' What is here called an 'anti-mimetic descriptive form' is best understood, I believe, as integral to the nature of mimesis. And we shall see that, however essentialist a poet Reverdy is, one can find instances of figural mimesis in his writings. After all, if the form of a text reflects a strictly speaking shapeless intention, the analyst's capacity to assess its formal aptness is nil. Auden's lines in his *New Year Letter* come to mind: 'Art in intention is mimesis,/But realised the intention ceases.' Where that is indeed the case, belief and speculation, legitimate but uncontrollable, take over from analysis. Only where there exists in reality some perceptible shape or form can it be reflected and therefore detected in a text. The articulations of logic may well be reflected in the form of a text, but they cannot be said of themselves, other than metaphorically, to have a shape. Our enterprise is thus confined to modesty, yet it involves the fresh reading of every single poem, a recognition of the consequent infinite variety, and the potential opening up of a whole new dimension to our reading.

P.N. Furbank has drawn attention to the pivotal effect in the last lines of Book 4 of *Paradise Lost* :

> The Fiend lookt up and knew
> His mounted scale aloft: nor more; but fled
> Murmuring, and with him fled the shades of night.

'The motion of a pair of scales is suggested, with "nor more" as its fulcrum. It is a definitive piece of mimicry...'. The very repetition of sound in 'nor more' intensifies our awareness of its function as a pivot between the upward movement of the initial gaze and the downward flight of Satan. We have seen an equivalent effect in Rimbaud's 'Mystique', where the palindromic thrust of the last paragraph describes a similar descent from the heavens to the abyss. Such a design is clearly susceptible of forms and interpretations which vary according to the subject matter of the text, the latter governing, as it does for phonetic patterns, the way in which the episode is understood. Candidates for such treatment are mirrors and other reflective surfaces such as still water, the description of mountains or valleys, of various thresholds in space or time (doors, windows, dawns, midnights), or the interaction of psychological profile and perceived realities. The shifts hinge on a word or phrase which thereby assumes crucial significance, whether mirroring a shape or advancing the logic of a case. The analysis of some examples will illustrate the importance of such features determining the architecture of texts.

The ninth and last of Verlaine's 'Ariettes oubliées' in *Romances sans paroles* carries an epigraph from Cyrano de Bergerac which recalls the baroque propensity to play on conceits of reversal: 'Le rossignol qui du haut d'une branche se regarde dedans, croit être tombé dans la rivière. Il est au sommet d'un chêne et toutefois il a peur de se noyer.' [The nightingale, high on a branch, which looks at itself in a river thinks it has fallen in. It is at the top of an oak and yet is afraid of drowning.] The text of the poem then re-enacts the interplay of inner and outer worlds:

> L'ombre des arbres dans la rivière embrumée
>> Meurt comme de la fumée,
> Tandis qu'en l'air, parmi les ramures réelles,
>> Se plaignent les tourterelles.

> Combien, ô voyageur, ce paysage blême
>> Te mira blême toi-même,
> Et que tristes pleuraient dans les hautes feuillées
>> Tes espérances noyées.

> [The reflection of trees in the misty river
>> Dissolves like smoke,
> While above in the air, among the real branches,
>> Turtledoves murmur.

> How much, O traveller, this wan landscape
>> Reflected your wanness,
> And how sadly in the high foliage wept
>> Your drowned hopes.]

This subtle variation on Amiel's notion that 'un paysage est un état de l'âme' [a landscape is a state of the soul] moves the eye from the uncertain shadows on the river's misty surface up to the dove-notes in the trees – real, Verlaine insists, however intangible and indeterminate the whole scene (helped by the openness of exclusively feminine rhymes). An equivalence of this outside reality is then postulated for the inner man so that two surfaces function as pivots in the poem. Within each verse the eye is taken from 'rivière embrumée' and 'paysage blême' to 'ramures réelles' and 'hautes feuillées' respectively; between the verses comes the shift from the perceived outer world to the perceiver's inner world.

The perceiver is here specified as a 'voyageur'. Such is also the case in a rare prose poem by Supervielle, 'Vertige':

> Le granit et la verdure se disputent le paysage. Deux pins au fond du ravin s'imaginent l'avoir fixé. Mais la pierre s'arrache du sol dans un tonnerre géologique.
>
> Joie rocheuse tu t'élances de toutes parts, escaladant jusqu'à la raison du voyageur. Il craint pour l'équilibre de son intime paysage qui fait roche de toutes parts. Il ferme les yeux jusqu'au sang, son sang qui vient du fond des âges et prend sa source dans les pierres.
>
> Calanques (Corse)

> [Granite and greenery dispute over the landscape. Two pines deep in the ravine imagine they have fixed it. But the stone wrenches itself from the earth in geological thunder.
>
> Rocky joy, you leap up on every side, climbing as far as the traveller's reason. He fears for the equilibrium of his inner landscape which petrifies everywhere. He closes his eyes until blood appears, his blood which comes from time immemorial and has its source in the stones.
>
> Calanques (Corsica)]

It will readily be seen that the same double effect is at work, the mental landscape mirroring the real one, in which the binary is dominant, shared as it is between granite and greenery, stapled as it is by its two pine-trees, divided as it is by the 'ravin' whose central letter, the hinge for its two syllables, outlines the relevant shape. The eye is rapidly drawn downwards into the depths of the ravine and the dislodged rock thunders down under the pull of gravity (appropriate in a collection entitled *Gravitations*). Emotion enters the poem with the first word of the second paragraph, and with it the clear upward movement of 'tu t'élances' and 'escaladant'. The traveller's mind registers the heady impact of this and vertigo threatens. The roots of his branching blood-stream probe the geology of that 'intime paysage' which, as it 'fait roche' in Supervielle's powerful phrase, reflects the outer world described in the first paragraph. That the upward and downward thrusts should engender the circularity of vertigo, itself mirrored in the last word's gesture back to the beginning of the text, reminds us that the linear force of gravity generates in the universe the circular or elliptical movements of planets and stars. The complex play of forces within the brief compass of the poem thus represents a continuity between fragment and cosmos, the part replicating in miniature the characteristics of the whole. The interaction between the panels of the poem's diptych draws attention to the importance of the pivotal expression which partakes of both the inner and outer worlds: 'Joie rocheuse'. That mid-point helps to define the form and nature of the parabolas traced around it, articulating the structure and encapsulating the essence of the poem's major metaphor and meaning.

A more muted effect is achieved in Reverdy's 'La Lutte des mots' from *La Balle au bond*:

La tourmente s'est égarée dans la lumière qui dépasse le toit. À midi, sans soleil. Les murs sont pleins de neige, sur un fond gris. L'œil s'arrête et cherche en vain une meilleure trace.

On a effacé les dessins qui animaient les parois descendantes. Quelques paroles s'élèvent affirmativement. Et le flot, trop haut, entraîne le bord où les herbes lissent la rive en cheveux bien peignés. Et tandis qu'à travers les rayons bleutés, les éclats tourbillonnent et s'élèvent, le silence tombe lourdement sur le sol sans se briser.

[The blizzard has lost itself in the light above the roof. At noon, no sun. The walls are full of snow, on a grey background. The eye stops and looks in vain for a better path.

The designs which enlivened the descending partitions have been effaced. A few words rise in affirmation. And the flood,

81

too high, pulls at the edge where weeds smooth the banks like well-combed hair. And while, through blue-tinged shafts of light, bright rays whirl and rise, silence falls heavily on to the earth without shattering.]

The pivotal words occur here at the end of the first paragraph: 'une meilleure trace'. They introduce, in a way confirmed by the subsequent reference to 'Quelques paroles' as well as by the title, the notion of writing against the erasing snowscape, envisaged as the striving for verticality against the snow's fall to horizontality. The literal snowstorm is the poet's metaphorical struggle with the blank page. Signs have been effaced from vertical walls, but 'Quelques paroles s'élèvent affirmativement', echoed later by 'les éclats tourbillonnent et s'élèvent', points of light against the dull backdrop, moments of effort, aspiration and even success against the weight of silence. If height is associated in context with both 'tourmente' and 'tourbillonnent', it is also inherent in their four opening letters: 'tour', literally scattered in '**to**mbe **lour**dement' (which phrase in turn contains all the principal phonetic elements of the opening noun 'tourmente' in the order in which they there occur), but ironically, perhaps even triumphantly, said not to shatter as it hits the ground. The phonic link between 'paroles' and 'parois', the reinforcement of 'trace' by 'dépasse' and 'effacé': these are not idle games with sounds. They consolidate the importance of their semantic association and confirm that it is less an existing parabola which is reflected here than a switch from one reality to another, each of which is the metaphor for the other, yet no less a shift from landscape to mindscape than in the poems by Verlaine and Supervielle we have discussed.

Mirrors hold such an obvious fascination for the poetic imagination that a reading public brought up on Lewis Carroll needs no reminding of their importance. They feature in many a Mallarmé poem and are at the heart of much of Cocteau's imagery, well known from his films. The mirror-image of reality is by nature different from that reality, not merely a reversal, and it is essential to think of being on both sides of the mirror at the same time, however difficult it might be to imagine what Pierre Mabille calls, in his study of the mirror in the imagination of the Surrealists, *Le Miroir du merveilleux*, the 'états psychologiques limites' [extreme psychological states] implicit in such a stance. When the usual reversed image is itself reversed, as in Magritte's celebrated painting of a man looking at himself in a mirror and seeing the back of his head, we find it profoundly disturbing. Everything becomes possible at the point of reversal, and we need to be alert to the many ways in which artist and poet might exploit its potential. That windows might serve similar ends is apparent from the many paintings by Magritte which, representing shattered panes of glass on the fragments of which the view beyond the window is imprinted, force us to question the nature of perception and reality. Metaphor has the power to perform a similar function, it too being the threshold between two represented realities. When we lose the certainty as to which reality is the tenor and which the vehicle of the structuring metaphor, we are perhaps ready to experience a disturbance equivalent to that of Magritte's paintings. It is then too, perhaps, that in our hunt for some point of purchase in the text, we notice the poet's strategies in greater detail.

The modern French writer whose poetics is most obviously built on the principles of Cratylian nostalgia and figural mimesis is Francis Ponge. As a foretaste of closer study, and since glass is much in our minds, let me quote an observation of his about the French word for a glass: 'j'aime assez que dans VERRE, après la forme (donnée par le V), soit donnée la matière par les deux syllabes ER RE, parfaitement symétriques comme si, placées de part et d'autre de la paroi du verre, l'une à l'intérieur, l'autre à l'extérieur, elle se reflétaient l'une en l'autre.' [I quite like the way that in VERRE (glass), after the shape (given by the V), the substance is given by the two syllables ER RE, perfectly symmetrical, as if, placed on either side of the walls of the glass, one on the inside, the other on the outside, they were a reflection of one another.] Such attention to the visual detail of the letters, combined with a selectively playful imagination, seems to fulfil the requirements of the quotation from Foucault with which I opened this chapter, although Ponge's reading of VERRE is not a calligram as understood in relation to Apollinaire. It does indeed blend the visual and verbal, making each indissociable from the other in the reader's memory. Yet it does so no more than Claudel's comment on the French for a mirror: 'Et *miroir* même quel dessin significatif avec ces deux rayons qui autour du vide central se répondent en éclairs répercutés.' [And *miroir* (mirror) itself, what a meaningful design with its two rays which, around a central void, echo one another with reverberating flashes.] Ponge merely continues the tradition of making observations about individual words and letters represented by Hugo (*Journal de 1839*), Mallarmé (notably in *Les Mots anglais*) and Claudel (*Idéogrammes occidentaux*, *Les Mots ont une âme* and *L'Harmonie imitative*), who already showed a considerable advance on those earlier writers who had largely restricted their observations and practice of imitative form to the phonetic. What Ponge does is to systematise such occasional remarks linking the visual and the lexical, erecting them into a poetic principle.

Plastic Ponge

Concentration on the rational discourse of language has brought the benefits of sophistication and subtlety of which we are aware. Any stance which asks us to view the alphabet not as a resource for significant words but as discrete designs inevitably appears perverse. Yet that very perversity is an integral part of the phenomenon which we have been tracing in these chapters, and Ponge ranges more persistently across the tracts of the figural than any poet from the 150 years of French poetry which they cover. His quest for re-enactment involves both the micro- and the macro-structures of his texts, and while this search for what he calls *adéquation* involves traditional elements of imitative harmony, its most striking innovation is the pervasive inventiveness of a figural mimesis which strives to rediscover or more precisely to forge a necessary rather than an arbitrary relationship between words and the object they represent.

Ponge's word for that endeavour is 'l'objeu', which itself plays on the interplay between linguistic process at its most stimulating and the object of its attentions. Alongside the echo of Mallarmé's designation of poetry as the 'Jeu suprême' stand the ideas of Freud in relation to both jokes and dreams, both of which enjoy, like so much modern poetry, a capacity for bewilderment and illumination. Something primal is scoured when we are invited to consider the potential of writing before the alphabet has congealed it and before the dream and the playfulness have been tamed by rational explanation. Not that Ponge supposes some pre-ordained necessity, divine or cabbalistic, in the formation of words. His Cratylian nostalgia, like that of all the poets we have investigated, takes the form of an attempt to create such a necessity out of the materials paraded in the dictionary. In an interview with Lois Dahlin, Ponge surmised that in ancient civilisations 'les mots et les choses étaient absolument identiques ... . Il y avait vraiment correspondance entre les sensations et le langage. Il est évident que nous sommes loin de là. La plupart des gens ont perdu ce sentiment, cette espèce d'instinct à la fois naïf, enfantin, et sage ...' [Words and things were absolutely identical.... There was a genuine correspondence between sensations and language. It is clear that that is far behind us. Most people have lost this feeling, this sort of instinct which is both naive, childish, and wise...]. If there is a lingering tinge of regret, a nostalgia for a mythical *illud tempus*, it resides less in the acknowledged arbitrariness of the relation between a word and the object it designates – indeed, Ponge expreses frustration that the word 'mimosa', for example, seems to him perfectly adequate to its meaning – or even in the attritions of morphology – which he can exploit by confrontation with earlier states of the word – than with the analytical syntax of French compared with Latin. Ponge's tendency to concentrate on nouns is a form of compensation for this regret, but it does not alter the importance of his decidedly visual approach to language and form and of his sheer inventiveness in this area.

In *Proêmes*, Ponge observes: '... il faudrait non point même une rhétorique par auteur mais une rhétorique par poème' [... you need not even one rhetoric per author but one rhetoric per poem]. That expresses in a nutshell the sense of overall shaping for a poem which escapes from the determinism of traditional form while also implying, through the use of the word 'rhetoric', that more than mere picture-poems are involved. In 'My Creative Method', indeed, a text dated 1948, Ponge enlarges on his comment, confirming his sense of the difference between what he is trying to do and what Apollinaire had done in *Calligrammes*, his own method purposely camouflaging but by no means reducing the iconicity of his texts:

D'une forme rhétorique par objet (c['est]-à-d[ire] par poème).
Si l'on ne peut prétendre que l'objet prenne nettement la

parole (prosopopée), ce qui ferait d'ailleurs une forme
rhétorique trop commode et deviendrait monotone, toutefois
chaque objet doit imposer au poème une forme rhétorique parti-
culière. Plus de sonnets, d'odes, d'épigrammes: la forme même
du poème soit en quelque sorte déterminée par son sujet.

Pas grand'chose de commun entre cela et les calligrammes
(d'Apollinaire): il s'agit d'une forme beaucoup plus cachée.

... Et je ne dis pas que je n'emploie, parfois, certains artifices
de l'ordre typographique;

— et je ne dis pas non plus que dans chacun de mes textes il y
ait rapport entre sa forme dirai-je prosodique et le sujet traité;

... mais enfin, cela arrive parfois (de plus en plus fréquem-
ment).

Tout cela doit rester caché, être très dans le squelette, jamais
apparent; ou même parfois dans l'intention, dans la conception,
dans le fœtus seulement: dans la façon dont est prise la parole,
conservée, – puis quittée.

Point de règles à cela: puisque justement elles changent (selon
chaque sujet).

[One rhetorical form per object (i.e. per poem).

Even if you can't ask each object to speak directly for itself
(prosopopeia), since that would produce all too easy a rhetorical
form and become monotonous, at least each object has to impose
some particular rhetorical form or other. No more sonnets, odes
or epigrams: let the poem's form be determined somehow by its
subject matter.

There's not much in common between that and (Apollin-
aire's) calligrams: the form in question is far more hidden.

... And I admit to using at times certain artifices of a typo-
graphical nature;

— and I also acknowledge that not every one of my texts
involves a direct link between its prosodic form, let's call it, and
the subject treated;

... even so, it sometimes happens (more and more often).

87

All that has to remain hidden, in the skeleton as it were,
never obvious; or even sometimes in the intention, in the
conception, simply in the fœtus: in the way in which the word
is grasped, preserved, – then released.

There are no rules for that, precisely because they change
(according to each subject).]

The only quarrel one might have with such a statement, which
affirms the centrality for Ponge of the principle of re-enactment,
is the rejection of certain traditional forms which might reason-
ably be found appropriate for certain occasions, and indeed Ponge
is not beyond using epigrammatic expression at times, for exam-
ple, to thrust home a point. The equivalence that he seeks
between the objects he selects for attention and the words in
which he tries to re-enact them is encapsulated in his formula:
'PARTI PRIS DES CHOSES *égale* COMPTE TENU
DES MOTS.' [TAKING THE SIDE OF THINGS equals
TAKING ACCOUNT OF WORDS.]

Ponge's best-known collection, entitled precisely *Le Parti pris
des choses* (written by 1939 and published in 1942), contains texts
which are in many cases short enough to visualise readily in their
entirety as objects produced in direct response to their subject-
matter. There is a gradation between those few which seem to
respond in an almost (but never completely) calligrammatic way
and others which correspond to the idea or ideas prompted in
Ponge's mind by reflection on the object evoked. The three para-
graphs of 'L'Huître' illustrate the former kind.

L'huître, de la grosseur d'un galet moyen, est d'une
apparence plus rugueuse, d'une couleur moins unie, brillam-
ment blanchâtre. C'est un monde opiniâtrement clos. Pourtant
on peut l'ouvrir: il faut alors la tenir au creux d'un torchon, se
servir d'un couteau ébréché et peu franc, s'y reprendre à
plusieurs fois. Les doigts curieux s'y coupent, s'y cassent les
ongles: c'est un travail grossier. Les coups qu'on lui porte

marquent son enveloppe de ronds blancs, d'une sorte de halos.

À l'intérieur l'on trouve tout un monde, à boire et à manger: sous un *firmament* (à proprement parler) de nacre, les cieux d'en-dessus s'affaissent sur les cieux d'en-dessous, pour ne plus former qu'une mare, un sachet visqueux et verdâtre, qui flue et reflue à l'odeur et à la vue, frangé d'une dentelle noirâtre sur les bords.

Parfois très rare une formule perle à leur gosier de nacre, d'où l'on trouve aussitôt à s'orner.

[The oyster, about the size of an average pebble, is more rugged in appearance, less even in colour, brilliantly whitish. It is an obstinately closed world. Yet you can open it: you must hold it in the hollow of a cloth, use a chipped, blunt knife, and go at it again and again. Inquisitive fingers get cut, and fingernails broken: it's rough work. Hitting it makes round white marks on its shell, like halos.

Inside you find a whole new world to eat and drink: under a *firmament* (technically speaking) of mother-of-pearl, the upper heavens slump on to the lower heavens, ending up as nothing but a pool, a viscous and greenish sachet, which ebbs and flows for eyes and nose, fringed around with blackish lace.

Sometimes very rarely a droplet pearls at their iridescent throats, giving something to adorn ourselves with.]

They mimic by their relative lengths the outside of the oyster with its larger upper shell, the smaller space inside contained in its smaller lower shell, and the tiny pearl occasionally found there. Phonetically, ruggedness is followed by viscosity and then by the plosives of surprise and delight at the rounded 'r's of the precious pearl. Semantically, the first paragraph determines size and colour but is largely devoted to recording attempts at opening the mollusc which, as a hinged bivalve, seems naturally to attract the crisp chiasmus of 'Les doigts curieux s'y coupent, s'y cassent les ongles'. Success reveals a whole new world to explore and enjoy, and we relish in our mouths and minds the phonetic and rhythmic texture of 'une mare, un sachet visqueux et verdâtre, qui flue et reflue à l'odeur et à la vue, frangé d'une dentelle noirâtre sur les bords.' Several senses are engaged here in the verbal feast, but our awareness of delicious displacement between mind and matter is highlighted rather in the final paragraph, where the pearl is both present and tantalisingly absent. For although the word 'perle' figures there, it is as a verb not a noun. All this well illustrates the 'objeu' and the particular 'objoie' to be derived from the process.

There is, however, a graphic detail which encapsulates the bivalve, namely the circumflex accent which appears on the title word. The attribution of particular iconic value to it would not be justified if it were not followed in several notable words by the sylla-ble 'tre': 'L'huître' itself to begin the text, then 'blanchâtre' and 'opiniâtrement' in the first two sentences, mirrored by 'verdâtre' and 'noirâtre' in the penultimate sentence. Otherwise, the circum-flex appears only on the last word but one, 'aussitôt', leading one to observe that all the circumflex accents in the text are equidistant from the central point, which represents the hinge of the oyster itself.

Ponge himself suggested as an afterthought at the 1975 'Colloque de Cerisy' devoted to his work that the considerable redu-plication of consonants in 'L'Huître' ('ss' x 7, 'pp' x 2, 'll' x 2, 'mm', 'ff', but not the 'nn' that Ponge finds there) 'rendent compte du côté feuilleté de la coquille de l'huître'. This smacks of rationalisa-tion. The phenomenon is as likely, if not more so, to reflect the shells around their hinge. Repetition of a more apparent kind, of which we have already seen some instances, is certainly very present in the text: 'grosseur'/'grossier', 'marquent'/'mare'/'rare'/'nacre', 'creux'/ 'curieux', 'franc'/'blancs', 'les cieux d'en-dessus s'affais-sent sur les cieux d'en-dessous' etc. Where such repetition is furthermore combined with the appropriate letter 'v', as in 'visqueux et verdâtre', we recognise the inversion of the circumflex accent and an additional visual feature in the formulation of a text which as it were encapsulates the qualities of oysterness. He kneads

– and needs – all the elements of language for the feast he prepares.

Somewhat less overtly calligrammatic is the text of 'Les Mûres' which none the less draws attention through metaphor to the relationship between the writing and typography of the poem and the blackberries in the hedgerow. In this case, it is the asterisks between the paragraphs which pointedly mimic the fruit. But time and again, here as elsewhere, Ponge wittily absorbs his material into his processing of it. Playing on the meaning of 'mûres' as noun (blackberries) and 'mûres' as adjective (ripe), he uses a synonym of the latter, 'fait' (used, for example, with reference to cheese), to suggest at the end that his poem is done. 'To a turn', one might think, but the overtone is different, and relates to another notation in the text, reminding one that in French a child 'fait dans sa culotte' [performs in his pants]: 'les oiseaux les apprécient peu, si peu de chose au fond leur reste quand du bec à l'anus ils en sont traversés' [the birds care little for them, so little remains after all when they have passed through them from beak to backside]. Aragon, in his *Traité du style*, had drawn attention to the double meaning of the verb 'faire', a particular example of the association made by child psychologists between creation and evacuation, and Ponge exploits the link here without vulgarity, tersely and effectively. Elsewhere, in his notes to *La Fabrique du pré*, he develops the idea, extending it to other forms of emission from the body, in which he sees an analogy to the solitary, disinterested creative process: 'l'expression peut être considérée comme une simple éjaculation: donc ne tendant à rien d'autre...' [expression may be considered simple ejaculation, aiming at nothing else].

When the mechanistic articulations of 'Pluie' end on 'il a plu', we cannot help but recognise in the choice of tense an opportunity which has been seized to derive the participle from both 'pleuvoir' [to rain] and 'plaire' [to please] so as to demonstrate the collaboration between the object evoked and the mental faculties which appreciate it. The mechanism of 'Le Gymnaste' is given so many animal connections that the gymnast is reduced to the level of mindlessness. The process starts by involving the shape of

91

letters on the page: we first see his head in profile as a capital G complete with moustache and goatee. Then his leotard reveals 'la queue à gauche' ['it' worn to the left] thickening one branch of the capital Y figuring his crotch. Active virility is kept strictly in check, however, by his need to keep in training, the rhythm of which is scanned by heavily-rhyming hexasyllables in a separate paragraph: 'Tous les cœurs il dévaste mais se doit d'être chaste et son juron est BASTE!' [All hearts he destroys but he cannot have joys being one of the boys!] Direct comparisons follow with monkey, worm and caterpillar as he contorts his body in the air during his exercises. And he ends as 'le parangon adulé de la bêtise humaine' [the lionised paragon of human stupidity], dragging those who cheer his physical feats down to his less-than-fully-human level. Too exclusive a concentration on the physical (and that includes the physicality of letters of the alphabet) is to be deplored. As Ponge observes in 'Escargots', snails, by fulfilling their duty as snails, leave a shining trail for men to follow: 'Mais quelle est la notion propre de l'homme: la parole et la morale. L'humanisme.' [But what is the proper study of mankind: language and morality. Humanism.] To man's 'excelsior' or 'fare forward' corresponds the snail's motto '*Go on* ', printed in English and in italics in the text so as to suggest the very shape of the shell and the snail's body straining forward from it.

'Le Papillon' displays clearly the characteristics of a text where an idea rather than an object governs the manner of writing. The idea is visualised nevertheless, the butterfly's flickering flight determining the phonetic, syntactic and semantic patterns of the text once the creature has emerged from the chrysalis stage. The plosives of 'papillon' invite other plosives and the image of a 'véritable explosion' from the chrysalis leaving the butterfly's body shrivelled between flaming wings. That image in turn is developed: 'Allumette volante, sa flamme n'est pas contagieuse' [a flying match, its flame isn't catching], or again: 'se conduisant en lampiste, il vérifie la provision d'huile de chacune [des fleurs]' [acting as a lamplighter, it checks the oil level in each of the flowers]. The flitting butterfly is seen on its way with an fluttering imitation of its flight: 'Minuscule voilier des airs maltraité par le vent en pétale superfétatoire, il vagabonde au jardin' [A tiny air-yacht ill-treated by the wind as a superfluous petal, it wanders about the garden]. The fondness shown for 'v's in this text, matched by their unvoiced sibling 'f', can fairly be considered, in the light of Ponge's visualisation techniques, as a diagrammatic representation of the butterfly's raised wings.

All Ponge's texts contain instances of detailed re-enactment (of which I have given a few examples in passing) which show both the variety involved and the consistency of the technique as an important adjunct to more familiar ones. In her book on Ponge's figural poetics, Annette Sampon writes: 'Ponge traite l'espace textuel un peu comme un espace plastique, il y dispose ses lignes-lettres dessus, il construit des formes épaisses, compactes, ou au contraire étalées, vastes, découpées.' [Ponge treats textual space rather like plastic space, placing his letter-lines on it, constructing solid, compact forms or alternatively ones spread out, vast, cut out.] It is easier, within a limited compass, to represent compact forms rather than extensive ones. Yet the principles he applied to the writing of the texts in *Le Parti pris des choses* remain valid in the later and longer works such as *Le Savon*, *La Seine* or *Comment une figue de paroles et pourquoi*, even if, as with Saint-John Perse's vast poems *Vents* and *Amers*, the overall shape cannot be perceived at first reading. The fact that they are less tightly organised and do not prompt critics to apply terms such as 'symphonic' is doubtless the result of a very different poetic mind at work, but it also stems in part from the greater fluidity of the substances evoked and the consequent appropriate indeterminacy of Ponge's chosen linguistic form.

The fact that Ponge so willingly commented on his creative processes and so readily made his drafts available means that we have a great deal of information at our disposal regarding his stated intentions. Once again, however, we are brought face to face with the problem of intention and realisation. If re-enactment remains 'dans l'intention, dans la conception, dans le fœtus seulement', how

93

is the reader to deduce it from the written text? It is only because of the consistency of Ponge's fascination with the process, and the evidence of texts where the intention *is* realised, that we make reasonable assumptions about the hidden presence of *adéquation* where it does not manifest itself.

The problem is far more acute in such a writer as Michel Deguy, who recognises the legitimate tendency in poetry to match matter and manner but sees poems, as he observes in *Actes*, as representing the 'configuration secrète de notre existence' and so veils in metaphysics the seductive shapings of his mind. Only the frequent comments of similar nature by many contemporary poets bear witness to the formative importance of Cratylian nostalgia in their thinking about the shaping of poems when shapes are no longer pre-ordained. Not since Ponge has a poet sought to explore to the extent that he did the realisation of the idea, yet the fascination with the visual shows in other ways, notably in the continuing production of *livres d'artiste*, in writings about paintings and painters, and in overt references to them in their poems.

Ponge's writings on painting are gathered in the volume *L'Atelier contemporain*, and the painter who emerges as a positive obsession for Ponge is Braque, whom he would elsewhere describe as his 'Maître de Vie'. One can readily understand the affinity between an artisan of words and an artisan of paint, each obsessed by simple objects and returning to them time and again to try and define their being and capture their essence in cycles of fascination. Yet just as Ponge endeavours to respect objects, recognising the essential difference between them and the words he uses to re-enact them, so he respects the difference between the painter's work and his own, and avoids assimilating the former into the latter as a mark of that respect. The delicate balance between art-history and art-analysis on the one hand and, on the other, the use of the visual arts as one pretext among others is worth observing in a selection of contemporary poets who in many respects show signs of withdrawal from the preoccupation with graphemic re-enactment which finds its culmination in Ponge.

94

New Harmonies for Old

A mong French poets of the last 150 years, the interest shown in the visual arts has been extraordinary. That interest has by no means diminished in the poetry of the last fifty years, which have seen a proliferation of references to paintings and other art works past and present and of collaborative ventures between poets and artists. In exceptional instances, poet and artist are the same person, and the aesthetic evolved through an intimate engagement with both arts is particularly instructive.

Rapid technological changes have excited creative interest but made developments harder to follow. Photography vies with lithography as a creative accompaniment to words, lithography now being considered more noble than it was when etching was paramount. Several magazines since *Minotaure* have striven to reflect an interactive ethos: one thinks of *Éphémère* with the group around Bonnefoy, Dupin, du Bouchet and Louis-René des Forêts, of the very different, glossy *FMR*, of *Derrière le miroir* and *Argile* around the art impresario Aimé Maeght, and a host of others. While Pierre Lecuire has continued to craft *livres d'artiste* in the Blake tradition of one-man books, and others, like Charles Tomlinson, combine the gifts of poet and artist in self-illustrated works, Roger Laufer has experimented on film with animation techniques applied to words and letters. Claes Oldenberg and Ian Hamilton Finlay are not the only artists to incorporate language into sculpture in their different ways, how far removed from traditional inscriptions on monuments. If Christian Dotremont has produced exceptional 'logogrammes' in which the very borders between word and image become uncertain, he is not alone in

95

experimenting in this area; while he seems to stay on the side of words, Pierre Cordier seems just to tip beyond them into the realm of pseudo-alphabets such as Michaux and the Lettrists devised and relished. Words and letters have indeed played a significant, integral and foregrounded role in painting from Cubism onwards, where before they had mainly provided ancillary information. In our everyday lives, our senses are assaulted by hoardings or publicity breaks between television programmes which popularise the interaction between word and image.

To name any names is invidious: it is impossible not to omit someone's favourite French poet from the recent period, and it is clear that major figures such as Breton, Éluard, Char, Michaux, Leiris, Queneau, Butor, Bonnefoy, Gaspar and Dupin deserve extensive consideration from the point of view of their relationship with the visual arts. Each befriended painters in his circle, reflected profoundly on the sister art, collaborated with painters and engaged with painting. If Char's decorated pebbles are less significant as art works than Michaux's dynamic graphical sequences, he none the less gave more time to writing about painting. How many poets' notebooks include more or less developed doodles interacting in ways to be determined with the words inscribed. How many painters have committed themselves to writing creatively. Certain twentieth-century movements, including notably surrealism, made both domains their province in the wake of such a nineteenth-century figure as Fromentin who cannot legitimately be confined to a single art form but has to be recognised exceptionally as master of two. To give priority to one is more usual, however interesting the minor accomplishment. Michelangelo the artist towers over Michelangelo the poet; and Delacroix the painter dwarfs Delacroix the diarist no less than Berlioz the composer does Berlioz the memorialist.

It is instructive to take some modern examples which show the range of interaction between verbal and visual preoccupations. By plotting them it becomes possible to situate a given writer from this point of view along a scale from the most extrinsic to the most intrinsic, using this information in conjunction with other considerations to define the poet's position and contribution.

André Frénaud, typical in so many ways of a left-wing intellectual born in the first decade of this century, has a poetic itinerary all the more exemplary for our purposes in that his work has never received the adulation enjoyed by more obviously original poets. Born into a provincial bourgeois family, educated at a church school but rebelling both against that education and his bourgeois background, he flirted with both surrealism and communism when they were fashionable but soon found their excesses insufferable. A modest civil servant, he fought for his country in the Second World War, was captured, and escaped thanks to false papers. His first volume of poems was published by Seghers in 1942 and greeted warmly by notable figures of the left: Sartre, Éluard, Aragon, Malraux. Supporting the Resistance, he did not, like Char, make himself outstanding in it, and after the war he continued quietly to amass his poems, publishing a second volume twenty years after the first, gradually making his individual voice heard more and more clearly among the many soloists of the last thirty years, and achieving recognition of a modest but solid kind.

As regards the poet's evolving relationship with the visual arts, Frénaud is no less emblematic of his time. His Burgundian bonhomie made him good company in the Parisian haunts of writers and artists. His long list of illustrated editions shows an eclectic range of collaborators including Dubuffet, Villon, Bazaine, Ubac, Beaudin, Léger, Estève, Vieillard, Miró, Masson, Chillida, Vieira da Silva, Asse, Alechinsky and Tápies. The styles of the artists are as varied as those of the poet, who adopts an exceptional range of personae to voice his concerns of the moment. Such paintings and sculptures as he evokes are often themselves made to present the world through the eyes of the subjects, but no predetermined stance is assumed other than an indefatigable questing interrogation of the world and its ways. Froment, Mantegna, Bosch, Dürer, Rembrandt, Cézanne,

97

Bonnard, Picasso and Miró vie with anonymous Romanesque sculptures to capture his attention and mould his reflections. He makes no pretensions to being an art historian but rather endeavours to encapsulate in appropriate form the thoughts inspired in him by the object of his gaze. Thus the short poems of 'Circuit au centre (en pays roman)' [Circuit in the centre (in Romanesque territory)], a series in *Haeres* (1982) evoking various elements of church architecture or decor, strive to capture moments of attention paid to tympanum, fresco or capital. The stunning Byzantine fresco of Christ in majesty which fills the apse of the tiny church at Berzé-la-Ville gives rise to the poem:

Ventre irradiant de Dieu

Du centre, éperdument, fourmillaient les étoiles,
une énergie, dans tous les sens, qui circulait,
sortie de nous, s'y réveillant, partout se dérobait,
ébranlement inouï, dénonciation solennelle
de l'Unique.

[God's radiating belly.

From the centre, frantically, swarmed stars,
an energy, in every direction, which circulated,
emerging from us, waking in us, hiding everywhere,
an unheard-of unhinging, a solemn denunciation
of the Unique.]

The more restrained Romanesque equivalent in the choir at Paray-le-Monial prompts a gentler piece:

Le grand dieu bien en place,
dans sa mandorle de gloire,
surveillait le sommeil
de l'agneau-enfant sur ses genoux.

[The great god, well-placed,
in his mandorla of glory,
watched over the sleep
of the lamb-child on his lap.]

These two poems well illustrate the way in which the visual is
entirely absorbed into the verbal in the best of modern poetry.
Due recognition is given to the shaping power of words in
sequence, account being taken of their phonology, structure and
juxtaposition so as to produce a text which in every way seems
right, whatever mysteries it inevitably leaves us to explore. The
similarity of construction in the paintings – the almond-shaped
framing mandorla in particular – gives rise to certain structural
similarities in the poems. The four lines of each reflect the
symmetry of the design, but in the first the very energy generat-
ed by the fresco thrusts the closing words into the *rejet* of an addi-
tional, seemingly incomplete line which endeavours, in form and
meaning, but with limited success, to hold everything together.
Punctuation interrupts the lines of the first poem, the syntax of
which is incisively disrupted into an energetic spikiness under-
lined by its plosives and sibilants. That energy produces longer
lines than in the second example, whose calm containment
bespeaks the enclosed and enclosing protectiveness envisaged.

There is no crude attempt here to produce a pictogram, nor do
Frénaud's statements on poetry and poetics suggest that he is
obsessed like Ponge by *adéquation*. Rather he assimilates the
lessons of a century of poetic practice and reflection on the
impact of the visual on formal constructions which no longer
accept traditional moulds. Even without a direct comparison
emerging between the poems just quoted (which appear fifteen
pages apart in *Haeres*), it is hard not to sense the overflowing vital-
ity of the one and the cradling power of the other, consciously in
response to the meaning of the words, unconsciously (before
analysis) to their texture.

It comes as no surprise therefore to learn that Frénaud's sensitivity to art has led him to write articles and prefaces as well as poems in response to work that appeals to him. This too has come to be considered a proper function for the poet to perform, lending his voice, as it were, to the mute canvas or stone. Baudelaire gave the stamp of respectability to the function through his extensive writings on art. Frénaud's most sustained writing in this area has been devoted to Raoul Ubac, on whom Yves Bonnefoy, who in many respects has inherited Frénaud's metaphysical mantle, has also written, but Bonnefoy has shown the sustained tenacity of the art historian in producing a series of major volumes on various periods and styles as well as on individual artists. Jacques Dupin has also been involved centrally with contemporary art throughout his career and it is not unfair to say that almost every French poet of recent years has been drawn to respond in one way or another to the impact of the visual upon him or her. Yet the overt nature of that interest has tended to divert the poet's attention away from the formal integration of visual stimuli into the shaping of responses to them in ways that are susceptible of objective analysis. As we have seen before, when forms of re-enactment stay within the poet's mind, the reader's efforts to link shape with stimulus remain conjectural.

Those conjectures can none the less be circumscribed and supported by noting the full range of a poet's involvement with the visual in general and matters artistic in particular, and the case of Lorand Gaspar seems in this respect extremely instructive, since not only does he write about contemporary art but is also a photographer of the highest order. What is more, there is evidence of a whole gradation of poetic responses to the visual, stopping short of the crudely pictographic but integrating its possibilities into more complex purposes. The formal variety of such a major collection as *Sol absolu* deserves close consideration from this point of view as from many others, and its opening text (preceded by a sub-title page containing the one word: 'SILENCE'), while not entirely typical, stimulates the reader's attention to this feature:

100

PIERRE   PIERRE
encore une
PIERRE

sable
illimité
RIEN

[STONE   STONE
another
STONE

sand
limitless
NOTHING]

The triangle of stones at the edge of the desert stands as the equivalent to the three blows struck at the opening of a French play to bring the audience to silence. Yet the disposition of the words on the page also suggest both the skull of a horned creature (the heraldic bucranion) emblematically apt at the threshold of a void – or at least an apparent void – which is both geographical and spiritual. If the Greek letter gamma is also discernable, it is a further reference both to antiquity and to the radiation of space. Those pulsars and quasars which traverse the cosmic void are as present to the scientist that Gaspar professionally is as are the plants and creatures that people the desert he explores. His reversal of traditional, western, symbolic expectations about the desert is in line with oriental notions of the void as utterly different from vacuity. The pictographic element of the liminary text is subsumed within far-reaching implications rather than indulged for its own sake. It alerts us pointedly, however, to the typographic variety of what follows, both in terms of the interplay of roman and italic, capitals and lower case, with regard to the blocking of words in groups on the page and to their variable spacing, and in

101

relation to the appearance of alien alphabets – Sumero-akkadian, Hebrew, Ugaritic, Egyptian hieroglyphic and Arabic – which, unless we understand their meaning, we see essentially as design. Yet such formulations are at the service of poetry, not a substitute for it, involving the visual but by no means restricted to it. Where such re-enactment takes its place in the gamut of techniques available to the poet, it is a key addition to the range but, on its own, neither a sufficient act nor a guarantee of excellence.

The recognition of this is no less apparent in the work of Bonnefoy, in whose poetry many a painting – by Tintoretto, Poussin, Constable and others – is directly or obliquely evoked. The very force of this extrinsic interest may well militate against any persistent excess of Cratylian nostalgia in his poems. The extent and intensity of his knowledge of painting lead him not to confuse the visual and verbal arts but rather to seek new harmonies between the utterly intangible and the most immediate. At the beginning of the century, Saint-John Perse had warned of the dangers of 'une génération à demi musicienne' confusing music and poetry to the benefit of neither: a little knowledge of the visual arts could by analogy make for facile poetry. In reinstating a strong element of narrative (a general tendency in recent poetry well analysed by Dominique Combe in *Poésie et récit*, Corti, 1989) and avoiding the blandishments of spurious visualisation, Bonnefoy revitalises a symbolism which establishes correspondences between concrete and abstract in his exploration of the spiritual. Of this there occur few clearer or more concise instances than in the final passage of *Dans le leurre du seuil* :

Des mots comme le ciel
Aujourd'hui,
Quelque chose qui s'assemble, qui se disperse.

Des mots comme le ciel,
Infini
Mais tout entier soudain dans la flaque brève.

102

[Words like the sky
Today,
Something which gathers and disperses.

Words like the sky,
Infinite
But suddenly entire in the brief puddle.]

That the closing line should remind us of the ending of
Rimbaud's 'Le Bateau ivre', with its 'flache' (a regionalism for
'flaque' [puddle]) is no surprise. In each case a whole imagined
universe is encapsulated in the microcosmic puddle which in turn
becomes an eye to envisage other departures of the mind.

The importance of Bonnefoy's work and the general recogni-
tion that it has received single him out for particular attention.
But as we have seen he is far from being alone in heralding a
marked change in the direction of French poetry since Ponge's
extreme practice of verbal appropriation. It may well be that the
phenomenon I have been investigating in these essays is now
essentially, in its more exclusive manifestations, a thing of the
past. Critics have come late to recognise it, but that very recogni-
tion may well be a kiss of death, since criticism often anaesthetis-
es the lion with which the poet struggles. Like the Romanticism
with which it developed, the principle of re-enactment may well,
however, take an unconscionable time dying. There certainly
seems no evidence yet that such a powerful force for coherence,
having effectively ousted the earlier shaping principles of rhyme
and regularity, is about to be replaced. If its lessons are learned
and blended in, as they are so notably and with such variety in the
poets we have investigated and many more besides, we can only
admire its exceptional value for cohesive flexibility.

Figures of Thought

Despite the basic reference to Plato's *Cratylus*, my primary purpose in this study has been neither philosophical nor linguistic, but literary. Highlighting the question of the shaping of poetry has allowed investigation of both detailed and general consideration of the visual in relation to the verbal. Attention to letters, accents and items of punctuation has shown that they participate in the overall economy of an attitude which specifically assumes and requires that notions of form and content be inseparably wedded. Such an attitude is crucial to the maker of poems when forms are not predetermined by tradition. Invention works interactively on a form-content continuum which produces that tingle of excitement by which the grateful reader recognises poetry.

By putting into relief an aspect of modern poetry which has, in my view, been insufficiently acknowledged by critics, I would not of course wish to suggest that it is more than an approach which supplements (but does not supplant) those which exist. It cannot of itself, however much it may help us to comprehend both certain well known instances and an underlying trend over 150 years, be the sole mode of analysis or the sole criterion for evaluation. Its value resides in the extent to which it makes us more alert and attentive to the textures and motivations of modern French poetry.

Towards the end of his study of jokes and their relation to the unconscious (volume VIII of his *Standard Works*), Freud uses the phrase 'ideational mimetics' to cover those physical forms of gesture and expression which we add to words in support of their meaning and suggests that if they were followed up they might be

104

useful in other branches of aesthetics. We cannot assume, however, that verbal expressiveness will invariably reveal authorial intention. The critical analysis of an artefact is subject to the limitations and consequent distortions of the critic conducting it. He or she is properly wary of attributing intentions to the author who in turn has privileged but not necessarily undistorted access to the recall of his intentions. The increase in the practice of interviewing poets about their own work doubtless affords many additional insights, but sometimes reveals a position adopted by the poet which is incompatible with the written evidence. If a dialogue of the deaf ensues, it may reveal more about the incompatibility of the two stances, creative and critical, than about the poetry under discussion.

That incompatibility has been exacerbated by the major trends in French criticism of the last forty years. When the traditional and entirely laudable desire to impose a pedagogical methodology on the processes of literary analysis assumes the mantle of scientific rigour, it implicitly fails to recognise that the object of its analysis enjoys by nature rather the dynamic instability of sand than the static firmness of rock. From the creator's point of view that instability is, on the contrary, all too painfully (if often inspiringly) clear at every stage: even the apparent solidity of the product is, shall we say, sandstone not granite, and eminently subject to continuing process. Hence the statements by several twentieth-century poets, from Valéry to Jacques Lovichi, that what is presented to public scrutiny is a state almost arbitrarily plucked from the many on-going states of a text. Hence too the successive versions of texts which the painstaking critic, no less obsessive than the poet though to different ends, is drawn to collect and compare. Temporary satisfaction must be set against a built-in dissatisfaction, but less with the idea that perfection is attainable than that flux is of the nature of life itself.

The search for poetic adequacy takes different forms when traditional verse is abandoned, but the shaping constraints are potentially no less creatively provocative than those, for example, of rhyme. Baudelaire like Wordsworth acknowledged that the search for a rhyme could divert some predetermined narrative from its ordinariness and produce an unexpected, heightened effect, proving the validity of the principle that a constraint freely assumed can be imaginatively liberating.

> Talk about a silvery moon
> and rhymes come all too soon,
> but say the moon is silver
> and you'll have a hell of a
> time
> finding a rhyme.

In recognition of the lack of rhyme in English for the word 'silver', my little jingle is meant to illustrate how frustration can lead to inventiveness. The same is true of the physical shaping of a poem, whether trivial like this or serious, according to criteria which only analysis of each individual text can determine. That there are certain underlying principles both for the formulation and for its analysis is something which these essays have sought to establish. Paying particular attention to a feature somewhat neglected by critics should not imply, however, either that it should oust other considerations unreasonably or that recent criticism has not shown some awareness of spatial form. Indeed that very term will remind many readers of the writings of Joseph Frank and the considerable discussion they aroused. Familiar and telling titles such as William K. Wimsatt's *The Verbal Icon* or W.J.T. Mitchell's *Iconology, Image, Text, Ideology*, herald the attention given to certain aspects of the phenomenon in the United States. Richard Bradford's *The Look of It: A Theory of Visual Form in English Poetry* has recently been added to that list.

In France much of the critical interest has been extrinsic, attaching to illustration, the *livre d'artiste*, aspects of typography and the like, or monographic, endlessly concerned with Apollinaire's calligrams, for example, to the exclusion of considerations of principle. The aesthetic centre has rather been explored by semioticians, regrettably using often rebarbative terminology which reduces one's confidence in the critic's capacity for literary judgement. But such is not in fact his purpose: our confidence may in part be restored by accepting that the semiotician is rather providing the literary critic with additional tools for his own differently orientated constructions.

Semiology was a medical term before being applied to language. Its metaphorical transfer from diagnosing symptoms to treating words as a system of signs was made in the late nineteenth century by Peirce in the United States and Saussure in Switzerland. Half a century elapsed, however, before first Saussure then Peirce caught the attention of French intellectuals at a time when the theory of structuralism had been borrowed and adapted from anthropology. In the way of fashions, extreme manifestations brought disrepute to more moderate forms which none the less revitalised critical approaches (such as that represented by 'l'homme et l'œuvre', whereby biography often became a substitute for textual analysis) which had previously held sway. Each critical 'ism' rapidly became a 'wasm', thus usurping, at a time when individualism reigned supreme among poets, the role that schools of creativity had earlier played. Both ancients and moderns provided ample ammunition for the other party to continue the quarrel and provide the bystander with saddened amusement. Intensity of debate gave way to inflexible tenets, the provision of grids for analysis which, in other than the most intelligent hands, left the object of study imprisoned, or quartered into identical chips. The text was relegated to being a pretext for the application of a methodology. Evaluation became an irrelevance, and some anaemic and lifeless journalistic report could be accorded the same treatment as the most subtle work of literature.

One of the most interesting ways out of this impasse has been afforded by scholars who have turned their attention to the interaction between different modes of creative expression. An increased interest in popular culture – stemming perhaps from the

107

late-nineteenth-century shift among historians from a general focus on the doings of kings and generals to the activities of the populace – has fostered the awareness and study of such phenomena as the carnival and, as in the case of Mikhail Bakhtin in respect of Rabelais, allowed the application of the concept to literature. Such democratisation finds both an outlet and a newly respectable object for study in today's popular culture which, even more obviously than carnival, involves both the verbal and the visual: cinema and television, posters and postage stamps, comic strips and video clips. The application to text-analysis of Peirce's categories of icon, image and symbol is singularly rewarding and warrants wider investigation. If the last two of these have tended to hold sway, I hope it will be seen from my series of studies that iconicity itself needs to be foregrounded for a proper balance to be maintained.

At a time when 'high' literature is mistrusted in so many quarters, and especially by students brought up in an audio-visual age, an approach to it through popular art can prove pedagogically valuable. I count Steve Murphy's work on *Rimbaud et la ménagerie impériale*, with its telling investigation of the relationship between Rimbaud's early poems and contemporary caricature, as being exemplary in this respect. The fact that some re-evaluation of the canon should occur under this pressure as under various others is salutary. Ponge now appears as the one major omission from C.A. Hackett's otherwise admirable 1952 *Anthology of Modern French Poetry from Baudelaire to the Present Day*. Segalen, so long sidelined into the *summa* of an exhaustive old-style French doctoral thesis and the enthusiasm of a chosen few, now flourishes as he should. Michaux, who once thought two hundred readers a feasible maximum, delights and surprises new generations of readers of paperback editions of his work and is a necessary point of reference for all students of modern French literature. Reverse discrimination is inappropriate, but the revelation of areas of legitimate interest and the consequent provisional re-ordering of a hierarchy of values is both natural and desirable, indeed all the more desirable for being natural.

108

That the act of poetry – and not merely poetic activity – should reveal itself as lying at the heart of our everyday urban lives by interacting with the very ordinariness of visual and verbal experience, reflecting its vitality and stimulating certain forms of its self-publicity, is scarcely surprising. What is surprising, and most regrettable, is to see how many intelligent critics fail to recognise the continuum between concern with socio-cultural phenomena in general – a fashionable trend in French studies – and the placing of the merest accent or comma in a text.

Insofar as audio-visual stimuli replace, in contemporary society, the respectfully printed word, orality adopts new strategies and regains territory lost during the latter's often supercilious primacy. Rap and rave may by some be ranked together with the insistent mindlessness of pop music, but could represent more of a growth point for poetry than the decorous maunderings that too often claim that title. Either way, to the extent that the book is bound for oblivion, the cycle in which French poetry responded for 150 years to the visual stimuli of formal re-enactment seems likely to be nearing its completion. Manifestations of the invigorating power of adequation will undoubtedly continue to occur, both in detail and in overall form. Yet just as we have linked the major moments of French poetry to crucial technological advances, the invention of printing and the industrial revolution, so it seems appropriate to recognise the new technological revolution represented by the computer and such developments as 'virtual reality'. The special status of language itself is called into question, increasingly viewed as a code among codes. Is the poet doomed to exploit only its inefficiencies, to play nostalgically with a dying prey for which he has in effect lost his appetite? I cannot and will not believe it. So long as the human capacity for inventiveness is enlisted more for creation than for self-destruction, dissatisfaction will remain a vital spur for enquiry into new forms, whether of poetry or of technology.

It would be foolish to predict what forms a poetic revolution might take. The phenomenon which we have endeavoured to explore occurs essentially between the age of the steam-driven press and that of the personal computer. The sheer acceleration in communications during that period is a measure of the excitement and the challenge involved. Alongside the technological revolution have been the social ones, and since implicitly the writer's motto is Terence's 'nihil humanum a me alienum puto' [I consider nothing that is human foreign to me], the poet has participated actively in those changes. The conservative may deplore lost privilege, the liberal continuing injustice, and each transfer to poetry some equivalent of that sociological regret. Yet other insidious forces are at work, and they go to the heart of creative form, by-passing all other considerations. Differences of personal attitude, amounting at times to irrational detestation, such as in Ponge's unmitigated hatred of Saint-John Perse, count for nothing when it can be shown that a corner-stone of both their poetics is the principle of re-enactment. Even so, the sheer variety permitted by the principle – 'les inventions d'inconnu réclament des formes nouvelles' [inventions of the unknown demand novel forms], as Rimbaud put it – means that it is not a bland recipe for sameliness but, on the contrary, a goad to the fulfilment of that vaulting dream of oneness between the word and the world which the *Cratylus* explores.

My own fondness for the practice of analysis rather than for theory will have been apparent enough from the present study. This in part, however, reflects the central simplicity of the principle I have defined and variously labelled Cratylian nostalgia, re-enactment, adequation or appropriation. Once seen, its myriad applications refract the shaft of illumination and split it into so many fragments that its centrality as a principle may tend to disappear. Patterns emerge, of course, but in effect each modern poem must be re-read in the light of the principle (which might even, as we have seen, illuminate elements of traditional verse) and considered both in its details and in its overall shape. The task is endless, but endlessly rewarding.

Select Bibliography

A comprehensive bibliography of the subject would run to several thousands of items, but by definition no existing study covers the ground from the angle adopted here. Listed below are those writings which have been most directly stimulating to my reflections over the years. Works of semiotic theory appear alongside others which deal more extrinsically, from different angles, with the relationship between the visual and verbal. Primary collections of poetry have not been included. Monographs are listed as examples containing focused analysis offering models for application to other poets or poems. Listed alphabetically by author, different types of study appear cheek by jowl, but watertight classification proved impossible as well as potentially misleading. Relevant periodicals include *Communication et langages, Communications, Critical Inquiry, Mélusine, New Literary History, Pleine marge: cahiers de littérature, d'arts plastiques et de critique, Poétique, Typographica* (partly reprinted in *The Liberated Page*, ed. Herbert Spencer, London: Lund Humphries, 1987), *Visible Language* (formerly *The Journal of Typographical Research*) and *Word and Image*. Note also *Yale French Studies*, 52 (1975): *Graphesis: Persectives in Literature and Philosophy*. Unless otherwise indicated, French books listed below are published in Paris and English ones in London. (U. P. = University Press.)

Bohn, Willard, *The Aesthetics of Visual Poetry 1914-1928*, Cambridge: Cambridge U.P., 1986
Bonnefoy, Yves, *Une autre époque de l'écriture*, Mercure de France, 1988

The Shaping of Modern French Poetry

Bradford, Richard, *The Look of It: A Theory of Visual Form in English Poetry*, Cork: Cork U.P., 1993

Bryson, Norman, *Word and Image: French Painting of the 'Ancien Régime'*, Cambridge: Cambridge U. P., 1981

Butor, Michel, *Les Mots dans la peinture*, Les Sentiers de la création, Geneva: Skira, 1969

Chapon, François, *Le Peintre et le livre*, Flammarion, 1987

Chénieux, Jacqueline, *Lire le regard: André Breton et la peinture*, Peeters, 1991

Christin, Anne-Marie (ed.), *L'Espace et la lettre: Écritures, typographie*, Cahiers Jussieu N° 3, Université Paris 7, Coll. 10/18, Union générale d'éditions, 1977

— *Écritures*, 3 vols, Sycomore, 1982, 1985; Retz, 1988

Collier, Peter & Robert Lethbridge (ed.), *Artistic Relations: Literature and the Visual Arts in Nineteenth-Century France*, New Haven & London: Yale U. P., 1994

Cook, Albert, *Figural Choice in Poetry and Art*, Hanover & London: U. P. of New England, 1985

Delaveau, Philippe (ed.), *Écrire la peinture (Colloque de 1987, Institut français du Royaume-Uni, King's College)*, Éditions universitaires, 1991

Deledalle, Gérard, *Théorie et pratique du signe*, Payot, 1979

Derrida, Jacques, *De la grammatologie*, Minuit, 1967

Foucault, Michel, *Les Mots et les choses*, Gallimard, 1966

— *Ceci n'est pas une pipe*, Montpellier: Fata morgana, 1973

Frank, Joseph, 'Spatial Form in Modern Literature', *Sewanee Review*, 53 (1945), repr. in *The Widening Gyre*, New Brunswick, N.J.: Rutgers U.P., 1963

— *The Idea of Spatial Form*, New Brunswick: Rutgers U.P., [1991]

Gandelman, Claude, *Reading Pictures, Viewing Texts*, Bloomington, Indiana U.P., 1991

Genette, Gérard, *Mimologiques: voyage en Cratylie*, Seuil, 1976

Gleize, Jean-Marie, *Poésie et figuration*, Seuil, 1983

Gombrich, E[rnst] H., *Art and Illusion*, Princeton, N.J.: Princeton U.P. & London: Phaidon, 1960

Hardison, O.B., 'The Poetry of Nothing', in *Science and Literature: A Conference*, Washington, D.C.: Library of Congress, 1985, pp.137-71

Hay, L. (ed.), *De la lettre au livre: sémiotique des manuscrits littéraires*, C.N.R.S., 1989

Hubert, Renée Riese, *Surrealism and the Book*, Berkeley, Los Angeles & Oxford: U. of California P., 1988

Kranz, Gisbert (ed.), *Gedichte auf Bilder: Anthologie und Galerie*, Munich: dtv, 1975

Lanners, Edi, *Le Livre des illusions*, Acropole, 1990

Le Men, Segolène, *Les Abécédaires illustrés du XIX⁰ siècle*, Promodis, 1984

Leroi-Gouran, A., *Le Geste et la parole*, 2 vols, Albin Michel, 1964-65

Little, Roger, '*Ut pictura poesis* : an element of order in the adventure of the *poème en prose*', in *Order and Adventure in Post-Romantic French Poetry: essays presented to C.A. Hackett*, ed. E. Beaumont, J. Cocking & J. Cruickshank, Oxford: Blackwell, 1973, pp.244-56

— *Rimbaud: 'Illuminations'*, Critical Guides to French Texts 29, Grant & Cutler, 1983

— *André Frénaud entre l'interrogation et le vide*, Marseille: Sud, 1989

Lyotard, Jean-François, *Discours, figure*, Klincksieck, 1971

McClatchy, J.D., *Poets on Painters: Essays on the Art of Painting by Twentieth-Century Poets*, Berkeley, Los Angeles, London: U. of California P., 1988

Marin, Louis, *Études sémiologiques: écritures, peintures*, Klincksieck, 1971

Martin, Henri-Jean, *Histoire et pouvoirs de l'écrit*, Perrin, 1988

Martin, Henri-Jean & Roger Chartier (ed.), *Histoire de l'édition française*, 4 vols., Promodis, 1982-6

Martin, Henri-Jean & Jean Vezin, *Mise en page et mise en texte du livre manuscrit*, Promodis, 1990

Massin, *La Lettre et l'image*, Gallimard, 1973

Mélot, Michel, *L'Illustration, histoire d'un art*, Geneva: Skira, 1984

Merleau-Ponty, Maurice, *L'Œil et l'esprit*, Gallimard, 1964

Metzidakis, Stamos, *Repetition and Semiotics: Interpreting Prose Poems*, Birmingham, Al.: Summa, 1986

— 'Visual Signals in Poetry', in *Understanding French Poetry*, New York & London: Garland, 1994, pp.71–86

Mitchell, W.J.T., 'Spatial Form in Literature: Toward a General Theory', *Critical Inquiry*, 6:3 (1979-80), 539-67

— *Iconology: Image, Text, Ideology*, Chicago, London: U. of Chicago P., 1986

Murphy, Steve, *Le Premier Rimbaud ou l'apprentissage de la subversion*, Lyon: Presses universitaires/C.N.R.S., 1990

— *Rimbaud et la ménagerie impériale*, Lyon: Presses universitaires/C.N.R.S., 1991

Paris, Jean, *Lisible/visible*, Seghers/Laffont, 1967

Peignot, Jérôme, *De l'écriture à la typographie*, Gallimard, 1967

113

— *Du calligramme*, Dossiers graphiques du Chêne, 1978
— *Typoésie*, Imprimerie nationale, 1993
Peirce, Charles Sanders, *Collected Papers*, ed. A.W. Burks, U. of Harvard P., 1960, esp. Vol. 2, pp.134-73
Ponge, Francis, *Le Grand Recueil: Méthodes*, Gallimard, 1961
— *Tome premier*, Gallimard, 1965
Quaghebeur, Marc, Jean-Pierre Verheggen & Véronique Jago-Antoine (ed.), *Un pays d'irréguliers*, Brussels: Labor, 1990
Queneau, Raymond, *Bâtons, chiffres et lettres*, Gallimard, 1965
Rothwell, Andrew, *Textual Spaces: The Poetry of Pierre Reverdy*, Amsterdam: Rodopi, 1989
Sampon, Annette, *Francis Ponge: la poétique du figural*, New York: Peter Lang, 1988
Scott, David H.T., *Pictorialist Poetics: Poetry and the Visual Arts in Nineteenth-Century France*, Cambridge: Cambridge U.P., 1988
Seaman, David W., *Concrete Poetry in France*, Ann Arbor, Michigan: UMI Research Press, 1981
Shapiro, Meyer, *Words and Pictures*, The Hague, Paris: Mouton, 1973
Solt, Mary Ellen, *Concrete Poetry: A World View*, Bloomington, London: Indiana U.P.
Souriau, Étienne, *La Poésie française et la peinture*, London: The Athlone Press, 1966
Spire, André, *Plaisir poétique et plaisir musculaire*, New York: Vanni; Paris: Corti, 1949; revised edition, Corti, 1986
Steinberg, S.H., *Five Hundred Years of Printing*, Harmondsworth: Penguin, 1955
Strachan, W.J., *The Artist and the Book in France*, Peter Owen, 1969
Uspenski, Boris, *A Poetics of Composition: The Structure of the Artistic Text*, Berkeley, London: U. of California P., 1973
Williams, Adelia M., *The Double Cipher: Encounter between Word and Image in Bonnefoy, Tardieu and Michaux*, New York: Peter Lang, 1990
Wimsatt, William, 'In search of verbal mimesis', *Yale French Studies*, 52: *Graphesis: Perspectives in Literature and Philosophy* (1975), 229-48
Winspur, Steven 'Reading a Poem's Typographical Form: the case of Paul Éluard', *Teaching Language Through Literature*, XXIII, 1 (Dec. 1983), 38-46
[Various], *De plomb, d'encre et de lumière: essai sur la typographie et la communication écrite*, Imprimerie nationale, 1982
[Various, ed. Anon.] *Iconographie et littérature: d'un art à l'autre*, Presses universitaires de France, 1983

Index of Names

INDEX OF NAMES